THE EXTRAORDINARY LIFE OF
CHARLES HUDSON VC

SOLDIER,
POET,
REBEL

THE EXTRAORDINARY LIFE OF
CHARLES HUDSON VC

SOLDIER, POET, REBEL

MILES HUDSON

SUTTON PUBLISHING

First published in the United Kingdom in 2007 by
Sutton Publishing, an imprint of NPI Media Group Limited
Cirencester Road · Chalford · Stroud · Gloucestershire · GL6 8PE

British Library Cataloguing in Publication Data
A catalogue record for this book is available from the British Library.

Hardback ISBN 978-0-7509-4436-6

Typeset in Photina MT.
Typesetting and origination by
NPI Media Group Limited.
Printed and bound in England.

Contents

List of Illustrations

MAPS

Acknowledgements

This book is based primarily on Charles Hudson's own very full 720-page journal which he wrote after his final retirement. His poems, none of which were published during his lifetime, were also of primary importance in assessing his personality and character. Secondary and most valuable sources were his letters to his sister in extreme youth, from the trenches during the First World War and from the ill-fated intervention in Russia. These were made available to me by my cousins, Roger and Patrick Crowley, who also helped in other ways.

The excerpts from Vera Brittain are included by permission of Mark Bostridge and Timothy Brittain-Catlin, Literary Executors of the Vera Brittain Estate, 1970.

I was also helped by the biography, *Vera Brittain: A Life*, by Paul Berry and Mark Bostridge (London, Chatto & Windus, 1996).

Sir John Stanier and my son Mark both read the manuscript assiduously and made many useful comments. Sir John Graham assisted me with his knowledge as a former ambassador to Iraq. Peter Hewlett-Smith helped with place names in France and Belgium. My cousin John Hudson and Major Oliver Hackett of the Sherwood Foresters Regimental Headquarters have also been very helpful. My secretary Vikki Tate typed the various drafts with her usual assiduity and good humour

Any errors are, of course, entirely mine.

Miles Hudson
2007

Author's Introduction

It is difficult for a devoted son to write a biography of his father without lurching into sycophancy, particularly if his father was touched by fame. Nevertheless the book will attempt to be objective. Charles Hudson's decorations and other achievements, recorded at Appendix A, were extraordinary. Whatever else he was or was not, he was certainly a very brave man. This book will examine details of his courageous acts – not only in war. It will try to establish his motivation in the light of his experiences in youth, his times and the society in which he was brought up.

Further, against the background of Hudson's life, the book will investigate the meaning of courage – that age-old virtue, almost universally accepted as such, but nevertheless full of ambiguities.

> The mean point between cowardice and foolhardiness? (*Aristotle*)
> The absence or overcoming of fear?
> A capital of willpower which is run down as it is used but is slow to build up again? (*Lord Moran*, Anatomy of Courage)
> Fear of letting down comrades or of being seen to do so?

And so on. There are many facets to courage – physical and moral.

The book will look at Hudson's poetry, a very vital part of the man exemplified not only in his own poems, which appear throughout, but also in his 'Perfect Lines' drawn from a wide range of poets and typed out in retirement on his own very old typewriter. These appear at Appendix B.

Then, Hudson the rebel, of which there are many examples: from deliberately failing his exam at Sandhurst, to constantly disobeying orders in war. His infuriating behaviour to his superiors in peacetime was probably a major factor, eventually, in him being relieved of his command of a division – as was his refusal to accept what he saw as wrong-headed authority.

Finally, to what extent did these aspects of his make-up – courageous soldier, poet, rebel – rely on each other in creating his character? Could one of them have existed without the other two? Where did his undoubted vast sense of humour come from? His lack of bitterness? And his all-pervading modesty?

Unless otherwise stated, all quotations in the book are taken from Hudson's own journal.

ONE

• • • • • • •

Nineteen Years

In the twenty-first century it is politically incorrect to talk about class. In the nineteenth century in Britain it was a central part of life and it was talked and written about a great deal, although not always directly. Charles Hudson's family would have been described as 'country gentry'. They had no pretensions to what was known as 'London society', to anything approaching aristocratic status or, indeed, to anything other than what they were. As Charles Hudson wrote in his journal: 'Subsequent to my first known ancestors, Adam and Eve, there is a gap in my family tree which, on my father's side, is considerable. A great-great-grandfather (Thomas Hudson, born in 1734) made money in the City of London trading with the West Indies but later generations consistently spent more than they earned.'

Indeed, his ancestors had resolutely turned their backs on trade, married people roughly of the same social status, and lived in various residences, some with small estates, almost always in the countryside. Their progeny had either stayed where they were in comfortable circumstances, joined the Army or Navy, or gone into the church. One became a barrister but did not practice and lived in Pau in France.

Another ancestor, Nathaniel Wright, had a sister who married Thomas Hudson's grandson and lived with her at Brabyns Hall, near Stockport in Cheshire. Wright raised and fitted out a regiment in 1803 and 1804 to defend his country against Napoleon, who was threatening invasion. This no doubt fine body of men luxuriated in the resounding name of the Loyal Poynton Worth and Bullock Smithy Volunteers (the Smithy presumably being the spot where they rallied to the cause). Such was Nathaniel's repute that he was presented with two gold-plated cups by the 'Lord Viscount Warren Bulkeley, the Colonel Commandant of the Brigaded Corps of Stockport Poynton Worth etc [whatever the latter letters may mean] as a token of the Sense he Entertains of his Loyal Liberality and Activity'. It was unlikely that any of this family went to university – indeed the author of this book may well be one of the first members of his family to have done so. Those who joined the Army went into their county regiment; there was no question of them joining either the Guards or the Cavalry. They managed to raise enough money to buy their commissions and when this, to us now, extraordinary practice was abolished, Hudson's father, Herbert, came into considerable obloquy because he arrived as the first officer to join the regiment by examination, 'in the opinion of his brother officers, particularly the older ones, this innovation would result in the Army going to the dogs'.

India featured very prominently in the lives of those who joined the Army, as many members of Hudson's family did. William James Hudson, Hudson's grandfather, born in 1821, became an Ensign in the 61st Regiment of Foot (later the Gloucesters) in 1842. After two years of garrison duty in Ireland his regiment was posted to India. Things were very different in those days. They sailed in five ships, the voyage to Calcutta taking over four months. William recounts in his diary that, having arrived, they marched to Cawnpore, a distance of 623 miles. It took them two months, their wives and families accompanying them sedately in carriages. They remained in Cawnpore for six months in extremely unhealthy conditions – eighty soldiers died of various afflictions. They then marched a further 400 miles to a military station called Ambala. After a long series of marches and counter-marches, the regiment was heavily engaged against the Sikhs at the Battle of Chillianwalla, which was a disaster as far as the English were concerned, but the situation was retrieved three days later at the Battle of Gujerat at which the Sikhs were defeated.

Not long after this affair William died of cholera. His last entry in his diary read, 'Feeling seedy.' The day before he had written, 'The NI [Native Infantry] have posted a notice on the barrack gate announcing that they will shoot their officers if their demands are not met – cheerful very.'

William had married the daughter of his colonel, Henry Burnside, and when the Indian mutiny broke out his brother, who was in the regiment, arranged for Burnside's wife, four children and French maid (who subsequently went mad) to travel 1,000 miles by boat down the rivers Sutlej and Indus to Karachi. It was the hottest time of year and there was little protection from the sun. The party had an escort for some of the way, but mostly they were alone with the Indian peasants who steered or rowed the small boat. The mother was six months' pregnant at the time. She was Charles Hudson's grandmother and must have been a powerful lady.

William's elder brother, Thomas, joined the 39th Foot (later the Dorsets), served in India and the Crimea, where he became Secretary to the HQP Hunt, started in Sebastapol after the war was over. (Despite much effort the author has been unable to discover what the letter P stood for.) William was also a steward at the Grand Military Steeplechase held on Monday 3 December, 1855 'before Sebastapol'. One of the races was for horses, 'the property of and to be ridden by officers of the French or Sardinian armies'. The race was for 'one mile on the flat'. Thomas's note on the racecard read, with obvious chauvinistic disdain, 'Eleven French started for this – a most amusing affair a French colonel winning.'

Charles Hudson's father joined the Nottingham and Derby regiment (the Sherwood Foresters) and became adjutant of the local volunteers in Derby. He was due to rejoin his regiment in India, but his wife refused to go. He left the Army and went to live in Newent, near Gloucester, where he rented a shoot and settled down to what must have been a rather humdrum life. He applied to rejoin the Army on the outbreak of the Boer War but, much to his chagrin, he was turned down.

Charles Edward Hudson was born on 29 May 1892, known as Oakapple Day because Charles II hid from a Roundhead patrol in an oak tree on 29 May. Charles's early life was clouded by constant rows and jealousies with his elder brother Tommy who, as the oldest son, was the apple of his parents' eyes. Charles and his sister Dorothy (Dolly) were thus thrown together and became fast friends.

Charles recalled that during the Boer War the

> small flagged pins stuck into the large maps in my father's study fascinated me then, as they did later during the Russo-Japanese war, but as far as I can remember my father never explained their significance and I never had any hankering after a military career. Life in the army seemed to me excessively dull, for it never occurred to me that there was the remotest likelihood of there ever being another war, and an army without a war seemed to me quite pointless and rather ludicrous.

Charles remembered the death of Queen Victoria and the deep mourning clothing which he and his entire family were dressed in as a result. At the time of the coronation of Edward VII as a young boy he had his first confrontation with the 'lower classes' when 'a crowd of rough-looking men surrounded the carriage in which we were driving and demanded funds for unemployed ex-soldiers'.

Charles recounts in his journal:

My father was a magistrate and as such he was asked to ride in the first 'horseless carriage' to appear in our neighbourhood. We children were taken to see this by our nurse and the nursemaid. The passengers sat facing each other. A number of speeches were made. A man carrying a red flag stood ready to mount a bicycle as the law required that all mechanically propelled vehicles should be preceded on the public highway by a red flag and he was deputed to carry it. I was in the charge of the nursemaid, and I was much annoyed at being dragged away from the car so that she could ogle the man on the bicycle whose name I learned was Joe. As the motor was set in motion after a few false starts, amidst the cheers of the crowd, a cloud of smoke and an all-pervading stink, the nursemaid told me that it might be a wonderful invention but however fast the car might go it would never catch up with Joe. Later I got to know Joe as a superman who wore a shiny striped black and white wristlet watch which fascinated me. His feats of strength were phenomenal. He was the blacksmith's assistant and wielded a heavy hammer all day long. In his spare time, moreover, he was the best quoits player in the village.

A further event which seared deep into his consciousness and which remained with him all his life took place when

a rather pompous ex-brother officer of my father asked me one day in a drawing-room full of people, as stupid adults will, what I was going to be when I grew up. Without thinking I announced that I was going to be a judge and ride a bicycle. Everyone present burst out laughing. This was too much and I was led away in a flood of tears. When I recovered, even at so young an age it dawned on me that my unconsidered remark had raised the hope in my mother's mind that I had unwittingly proclaimed my future destiny. Later she carefully explained that I would have to become a barrister before I could become a judge. At the time I was far more interested in the bicycle.

This event was to spark an amused echo in the verse he wrote later:

A Child's Dream

If I could have my wish what I would be
I'd choose, I'd choose a monkey on a tree,
A feckless creature, one would think, but free
But then perhaps he thinks the same of me –
I'll try again, a great man, let me see,
A learned man as busy as a bee,
A scientist or doctor with a fee
So great he never lacks the things that he
most wants, a bike or sausages for tea.
A man of action on the land or sea
Or in the air, perhaps I've found the key –
a hero, that's the ticket, yes, that's me.
But something's missing, what then shall I be,
There's always something else puts in a plea
Sometimes a tweedle dum and then a dee,
but in my heart there is a constancy –
I'd like to stay a child eternally,
But, sadly, I will have to wait and see.

When Charles was about seven years old a great change occurred in his life. His father inherited a considerable income from family land in Derbyshire. The lease of the house in Newent ran out at about this time and he bought a much larger house with land attached called Bereleigh, near East Meon in Hampshire. It was the first time Charles had come across electricity and he got into trouble for running from room to room switching the electric lights on and off.

No longer were we confined within the narrow limits of a small walled garden and daily afternoon walks under the close supervision of a nurse or governess. We could go as far as our legs would carry us on our own land. The so-called Long Drive was said to be a mile long. My brother went off to a preparatory school in Sussex where I later followed him. Bicycles appeared and ponies. We played cricket with boys and men belonging to the estate; we trudged the fields with my father and a keeper looking for plovers' eggs. We had hideouts in the woods. We played tennis and croquet. Even lessons became less boring for a new governess appeared who knew how to conduct them. At Newent we had suffered under a series of impossibly incompetent and elderly spinsters, whose sufferings were only exceeded by our own.

When Mustard, a fiery little pony, arrived, my life became less carefree. I had little control and riding soon became an agony. Two experiences stand out, the first when riding along the edge of a wood I came round a corner and saw, a few hundred yards away, a light single-horsed trap. A man with it was just throwing some rabbits into the back. When he saw me he shouted and ran round to jump into the driving seat.

My father often talked of the poaching that went on, and I realised with a spasm of fear that I had come on poachers. Three more men appeared out of the wood and stood there awaiting me. They looked rough and tough-looking customers. Much as I would have liked to turn tail and bolt, for many unpleasant stories of the kidnapping of children by gypsies leaped to my mind, I felt this would be too ignominious. With beating heart I rode up to them and demanded what they were doing.

Their jeers and scorn reduced me to a state of confused impotence and ended with a final insult when one of the men, seizing the bridle, turned my pony round while another caught him a sharp crack with his whip. As I held on for dear life, my pony entirely out of control, the derisive cheers of the men in my ears completed my humiliation.

About this time my father became very ill, and in our last summer holidays at Bereleigh a tutor was engaged, ostensibly to give my brother extra tuition but mainly to keep us in order. I soon became his passionate admirer. He was in fact still an undergraduate, but to me he seemed an oracle of age and wisdom. . . .

One day Mr Johnson (later to become a very high-church and disappointingly dull young curate in a fashionable part of London) accompanied me out riding on his bicycle. Our progress down a main road – I on the broad grass verge and he in the roadway – developed into a race. I was soon out of control and he, not realising this, shot ahead. My pony, recognising a side road as the way home, swerved and deposited me on my head in the ditch. My poor young tutor hunted distractedly for his charge but since I was unconscious and out of sight he failed to find me.

I came to in a strange and enormous double bed in a room that seemed to me to surpass all normal standards of expensive elegance and luxury. My first reaction was to think how surprised people would be to know that Heaven was really like this, my second was that it was all very fine but I would really rather be in my own ugly little commonplace room at home. A very heavily starched and business-like professional hospital nurse and a splitting headache soon convinced me that I was still earth-bound.

It turned out that I had been found before the search party, headed by my father, had set out, and had been carried unconscious into the house of a very wealthy Jewish family who had recently appeared in the neighbourhood. I suffered no after-effects from my adventure, and our life soon after became over-shadowed with my father's serious illness. An operation was performed upon him in the house by a London surgeon. The medical ruling subsequently given was that he must lead a very quiet life and should live by the sea. We went to Bournemouth and our whole scale and mode of living changed from that of a country to a suburban life – a poor exchange.

As happened to virtually all boys of his background, when he was eight years old, Charles was sent to a preparatory school – Fonthill near East Grinstead, Sussex. He was very close to his sister for reasons already explained and three letters from him to her have survived. Although not always clear – what is meant by 'cobbed'? – they exemplify much of the atmosphere in which children from his background lived at the turn of the century – and indeed in many cases still do.

Fonthill
East Grinstead
Sussex
Sunday, 26 February 1905

My dear Dolly,

I am sorry I did not write before. The chapel is not finished yet. It is taking an awful long time. I am looking forward to Nigger coming next holidays. My group has all been cobbed and so Walter would not let me into the Club. There are fifteen chaps who have got chicken pox. They are all singing or shouting rather in one of the bedrooms. I will get it soon I expect. It is pouring with rain now. We have had a little snow lately. I do not know whether I am in the eleven. We would have a match on Wednesday but chicken pox broke out on the Tuesday which was rather bad luck. We won't have any matches for a good time yet. Nothing more has happened about it, you know. It was probably all rot. I here [sic] you get a good many bike rides. We had boxing yesterday.

Love to all
From your loving Charlie

Fonthill
East Grinstead
Sussex
11 February 1906

My dear Other Half,

I wish I could join with you and make a whole. I am getting on with my work pretty well for the master I do with. I am doing Euclid now because if I try for the Navy I have to do it. I like it. Do you think you could scrape together some eggs, not too common because I am promised a collection of moths and butterflies. I wish you could. What have you been doing lately! I have had a letter from Nigger lately. He sent some photographs, the ones which you and I took out on the veranda. One of the masters was biking back from East Grinstead, as he came down a hill just near Fonthill his lamp went out, so he did not light it because he was so near home, then he saw somebody biking towards him. When he came to the other man he jumped off and told him to get off too so the master asked him what he wanted. He said he wanted the master's name and address for riding without a light. The man on the other bike was really a police inspector. My diary is getting on very well, is yours?

Love to all
From your loving Charlie
PS It is Ashton's birthday today. We are going to have a conjurer soon, his present some books, £5 10s was given by the boys for it.

Fonthill

East Grinstead

Sussex

Summer Term

My dear Dolly

It doesn't seem as if it will ever stop raining. There are four new boys, two new masters. The tribal Alliance has got a band of 8 boys, 3 of which are secret spies. We are fighting another band, one of our spies pretended to be in theirs and found out all about their spies and plans. We have got a secret cipher of our own. We are going to have boxing. We did gym yesterday. The dancing class is jolly nice, we do not do exercises or steps or that beastly stuff. I hear you are going to drawing class and to *Alice in Wonderland*. The master who teaches boxing held the championship for two years on board the *Britannia*. How are the dogs and bird? Mind you water the caterpillar. We played hockey this afternoon. I hope you like the drawing lessons.

Love to all

From your loving Imp

There were two headmasters. They were brothers. One, married, lived in a separate house in the school grounds. The other, unmarried, lived with his sister in the school and it was this man, a sadistic monster, who was to have an enormous and unquantifiable effect on Charles's character. The whole school was frightened of him, but for four boys, including Charles, fear was altogether too weak a word.

We were kept in a state of terror in the knowledge that not only did he loathe the sight of us but that our very presence brought out the worst and most cruel side of his sadistic nature.

His sister tried to console me by explaining that he suffered terribly from gout in the head and could not sleep at night. It never occurred to me to wonder why I should be picked out to suffer as a result of his misfortune. His persistent bullying soon convinced me that I was the fool he made me out to be. I never told my parents about the bullying headmaster, partly because I was too ashamed of my own failure, partly because to do so would be an unpardonable offence against the rigid code of a schoolboy's honour, in which 'to sneak' even on a master was beyond the pale.

Richard (we actually called the two heads by their Christian names though the other masters we 'mistered' in the normal way) took all Latin classes in the school. It was during these classes that he seemed to take a delight in tormenting me. The technique was nearly always the same. He would pay little attention to me until nearly the end of the period. He would often hover over me and then at the last moment pass me by. But the inevitable moment would come. He would bend over me and at once I would be almost paralysed with fear.

He would make some superficially jovial remark in my ear, but I knew it to be ominous and charged with a faint sarcasm in connection with some previous painful incident. Slowly he would read my miserable effort to render some simple passage into Latin, and when he had found some obvious mistake the hectoring would begin. 'Do you know that such and such a noun is feminine?' he would say. Trembling, I would reply I didn't know. He would pick up my exercise book and turn the pages back. He would find either the same error corrected or written as it should have been. In either case he could point out that I must have known and that I had lied in saying I didn't. I would be told to go to his study and there await my doom. I used to try to pretend to the other boys that I did not mind being beaten, and to prove it I used to steal chocolates which Richard kept in a drawer in his room for distribution as prizes. These I would give to my friends when I came out. Richard's beatings were not formal affairs of so many counted strokes.

One day he was laying about me with more than usual vigour and working himself into a fury at my failure to get a single word right under the threat of the cane, when there was an urgent knock at the door. He threw the cane into a corner as his sister entered. I could not fail to realise she had come in only to rescue me. It was after this that she told me of Richard's gout.

Richard had told my father that I would never pass any Public School entrance examination unless I had extra tuition in Latin, and so my father had to pay for my extra hours of torment.

After prayers, every boy in the school had to pass Richard on his way to bed, shake hands and say 'Goodnight, Sir'. When my turn came he might refuse my proffered hand and say, 'I'll see you later.' That meant I would have to go into a small room in the private part of the house and await his appearance. Three other unfortunates accompanied me and we would be set an exercise while Richard had dinner.

The culminating horror of these private classes came one Saturday night. I had been beaten that morning and could only kneel on my chair. Richard came back to us in a joyful mood, apologised for his lateness, explaining he had some old boys to dine who had been most amusing companions. He looked over the other three boys' work perfunctorily and sent them off to bed.

I had had a dreadful day and was in a state of collapse and quite unable to concentrate. All I had to show were a few lines of tear-stained and quite illegible writing. Richard stood behind me breathing heavily and alcoholically down my neck. He began thumping me in the back, his thumb between the fingers of his clenched fist, pouring out imprecations. I slipped from my chair and tried to run round the table but he caught and shook me. I thought he would kill me in his now uncontrollable rage. Then suddenly he threw me from him and rushed out of the room.

Soon after I heard men's voices, Richard's among them. They were coming out of the dining-room. I heard the drawing-room door open and the sound of women's voices and laughter, then the door shut. My overwhelming need was to go to a lavatory. I tried biting my lips in an effort to control myself, but it was no good. I had just slipped out into the hall intending to make a dash for the lavatory near the front door when I heard footsteps. Before I could get back, Richard appeared at the top of the stairs, a cane in his hand. As he entered, I rushed into a corner of the room, and, unable to control myself any longer, the worst happened.

'You dirty little brute,' he said. 'Get out of here, go to the matron and tell her from me you have got to have a bath.'

I fled before the lashing cane. In those days we had round tin baths in our dormitories on bath nights. The other boys in my dormitory were mostly asleep but matron herself brought a candle, filled a bath and told me to wash quickly and get into bed.

When she returned she found the water red with blood. Horrified, she examined my lacerated behind. Realising she was very upset and angry I begged her not to tell Richard. The door of the dormitory was always left open and it was not long after I crept into bed that I heard her tiptoeing along the passage outside and up a short flight of stairs to an assistant master's room. Creeping out I went to the bottom of the stairs and listened.

The door above was open and I could hear enough of the conversation to gather that matron was almost hysterical and that Mr Vavasour, an assistant master, was urging her to go to bed, assuring her that he would see Richard in the morning.

I never learned what happened, but for the rest of that term Richard left me in peace. Mr Vavasour did not return to the school for the next term. I never saw him again, but I heard later that he was running a most successful school near Midhurst. I had good reason to be grateful to him.

After I left, something similar must have happened for, if my information was correct, an angry parent told Richard he must either retire or face a charge of assault. He chose the former alternative, and handed over the school to his brother.

This whole episode must have had a vast and permanent effect on Charles's character. We can all remember with great clarity situations and events in our youth which were defining moments in our development although often to an outsider they may appear to be insignificant. But to a 10- or 11-year-old boy from a secure, although (except for his sister) perhaps a little frigid, home these barbaric events must have been totally horrific. The fact that he did not tell anyone about it at the time was not surprising – the reluctance of children to tell their parents about their personal problems persists now and probably always will. Whether this traumatic affair had a direct bearing on his subsequent behaviour and, if so, to what extent, we will examine later.

Before going to his public school, Sherborne, where he remained from 1905 to 1910, Charles attended an interview in London with a view to going into the Royal Navy. There was no question of his going 'into trade'; he thought he was too stupid ever to qualify for a 'learned profession' and his brother, who had joined the Army, strongly dissuaded him from following in his footsteps. He failed the interview, learning many years later that it was decided, not surprisingly in the circumstances, that he was 'of too nervous a disposition'.

Charles's recovery of self-confidence was undoubtedly, in part, due to the environment in which he found himself at his new school, Sherborne, which his brother and his father had attended. Not knowing what to do with himself having failed the Navy, and very doubtful of his academic potential, he had joined the Army Class where he was taught by Trevor Dennis, an ex-member of the Sudan Civil Service. Schoolteachers, male and female, do not always realise what they can do for their pupils. Dennis transformed Hudson's view of himself and of his academic abilities.

Until he arrived I had always imagined that I was only capable of floundering about at the bottom of any class and could not be expected to do better. Though his immediate concern with me as a pupil was to teach me mathematics, he lit up for me a far larger area of interest. I was probably at an age at that time when a boy's mind is apt to open out, and lessons become education, but I had him to thank for the change that came over me. Intellectually I became alive. I had always been unable to memorise anything and I had thought that this was evidence of stupidity. Dennis showed me that the brain was not just a factual recording machine, nor was it only of use through its power of logical reasoning but that an understanding of a mathematical, and of any other, problem, could be reached imaginatively. Until in fact a proposition was so comprehended it was unlikely that a realistic solution could be found. Dennis himself never attempted to put these ideas into words. Still less did I attempt to do so myself, but nevertheless he did impress on me that I was seeking to find for myself a good deal more than an accumulation of factual knowledge that would enable me to pass examinations. This gave me an entirely new interest in life, and an exciting one.

So much for Charles's mental inferiority complex but, of course, the same disability affected the physical side of his character and Sherborne gave him the opportunity to overcome this besetting and most distressing problem. The game of rugby was a central feature of life in Sherborne. It was believed that characters were formed on the rugby field. Being part of a team and the sheer physical aspect of the sport were calculated to bring out the best in a growing boy. Indeed this ethos was thought to play a large part in the extraordinary growth of the British Empire. Be that as it may, Charles found himself, as far as his mastery over fear was concerned, on the rugby field. His house fielded the weakest team in the school and was to play the strongest in a house match. The fullback suddenly became ill and, to his horror, Charles was told he had to take his place. In the first half the score mounted to astronomical figures.

In the second half, the opposing team obviously began to toy with us, passing the ball between them without making any attempt to increase their score. This contemptuous treatment enraged me. Tired and battered as I was, I forgot my fears. A new and previously unknown surge of energy and determination possessed me, and I launched myself against all comers with the restless fury of desperation.

As I stumbled exhausted from the field the opposing housemaster, a giant of the rugby field in his day, a captain of England, the great G.M. Carey, congratulated me in glowing terms. I could hardly believe my ears. But I was still more astonished and impressed when a friend of mine in Carey's House told me that the whole house had been severely lectured on the failure of their team to play all out whether they happened to be winning or not, and that I had been mentioned as an example of unremitting effort regardless of the score. From that moment of realisation that I was able to master my own physical fear, I recovered my nerve.

It will be argued later in this book that Hudson's remarkable record in both world wars was due to three critical aspects of his character: mastery over physical fear, an imaginative response to situations and a growing intellectual curiosity. For the moment, though, Charles's character was still being formed at Sherborne School.

The third man at Sherborne who made a deep impression on me, though not so favourably, was the Headmaster. My Housemaster, a clergyman, had prepared me for confirmation, and I can remember little of his approach to the subject, but before the actual event I was summoned to a personal interview with the Head.

Though full of religious fervour as a result of my preparation for confirmation, I went to the interview in considerable trepidation for the 'Chief' (as the Headmaster was called) was a very remote, awe-inspiring and at the same time an almost saintly figure.

Almost the first question that he asked me was whether I ever listened to or told improper stories. I was very taken aback but, regarding the occasion as one which nothing else than the whole truth should be told, I said I had been guilty in this respect. In fact, as I was later to learn, my idea of unclean stories was confined to little more than schoolboy vulgarities.

My shamefaced admission brought down on my head a lecture that appalled me. I deserved to be an outcast from any decent society. I was soiling not only my own soul but those of all with whom I came in contact. Only through the grace of God could I hope for redemption. In fact, he said, it was very doubtful whether I could be regarded as fitted for confirmation at all.

Later I asked a friend who had also been interviewed if he had been asked the same question. To my astonishment he told me that he had, but had not been such a fool as to say he was guilty. I did not know whether to admire or condemn his resolution.

Honest or naïve – who is to say?

Hudson had not expected to pass into Sandhurst, but to his and everybody else's astonishment he succeeded by a considerable margin. He had no particular wish to join the Army but he had no other ideas and to Sandhurst he went. The course at Sandhurst was for two years with an examination at the end of the first year which had to be passed. Failure meant repeating the first year, a most unpleasant and daunting prospect.

Shortly before the examination was due he received a wire that his father was dying. He arrived too late to find his father conscious and death quickly followed – a terrible blow to the young Hudson. He was told that his father had been unable to leave any money to him, or to his sister, because everything had been entailed on his elder son, Tommy. He had asked Tommy to make Charles an allowance of £100 a year, considered to be the minimum income necessary for an officer in the Army. Tommy had been prepared to fulfil his father's wishes, but Hudson stubbornly refused to become beholden to his brother and would not accept the allowance under any conditions. His family urged him not to be so stupid and he realised that the only way out of his difficulty was to fail the pending examination. The first paper was military history, his best subject. He deliberately wrote rubbish in answer to the first few questions and then left the room. That seemed to be the end of his military career.

There was a whiff of what can only be described as bloody-mindedness in this action. There was heavy pressure on him to take a certain course of action which went against his deepest instincts. He did not care what the repercussions would be: he was not going to be beholden to his brother, come what may and that, as far as he was concerned, was that. We shall note several similar actions later in his life, notably in 1941. This attribute of refusing to defer to what he saw as wilful, arrogant and misguided authority may also have stemmed from when he was sadistically bullied by his headmaster at his preparatory school. He had overcome his physical fear and his mental inferiority complex at Sherborne School and this had given him the self-confidence to stand up to authority in any guise.

Sandhurst was a tonic in many respects. Self-discipline and a sense of duty were firmly inculcated, and for the first time I came in contact with authority as exercised by men who were not themselves brought up in public schools and universities, non-commissioned officers, a new and refreshing experience.

The boys, too, were far more diverse in character and attainments than at Sherborne, coming as they did from many different schools and home environments.

Sherborne had taught me very little of the impact of competitive life on various kinds of individuals, and the effect of ambition on many. Sandhurst began to open my eyes to this new aspect of life in the community. By nature retiring, I made no effort to push myself forward, but in fact had I done so I would not have risen above average in any respect. I did occasionally represent Sandhurst at hockey and tennis, but did not become a regular member of their teams, which in any case were not regarded as being of much importance at the time.

The only other event at Sandhurst of some importance in his later life was that one of his contemporaries at the establishment was Harold Alexander, whom he admired immensely both for his general demeanour of amused detachment and his first-class brain. Little did he know that he was to go to France in 1940 as a brigade commander with General Alexander as his divisional commander and that they were to work together with success, ease and mutual regard.

After Charles's father's death, his mother moved to a small house near Haslemere in Surrey. There he fell in love, but he was 'too young and callow', as he put it and his love was unrequited. He scanned the 'Wanted' columns of the newspapers for work, initially without success. Meanwhile he went as a learner to an apple-growing farm in Herefordshire. He had £500 of his own left to him by a grandmother and he managed to exist on that for a time. However, he had no capital and his future was, to say the least, uncertain.

He had one extraordinary experience at that time. Having been told that there was no train due he, a fellow pupil and a child, walked through a railway tunnel to avoid a long and arduous walk. In fact, when they were half way through the tunnel,

We heard a distant rumbling. At first we thought it was thunder, but it soon became obvious that a train was approaching. The thunderous noise became a roar. My brother pupil found a built-in workman's niche in the sidewall and shouting at me dragged the girl in beside him. By the time I had groped my way over to them the train seemed almost on top of me. The glare from the furnace of the engine lit up the niche and I realised that there was no room for me nor was there time to find another niche. . . . I threw myself down between the rails and pressed my face between the sleepers. As I lay trying desperately to flatten myself out, the train rumbled over me. . . . It was a hair-raising experience for us all.

Eventually Hudson's perusal of the 'Wanted' columns was successful and, through an agency, he obtained a job with a tea-planting establishment in Ceylon. The vacancy was not immediately available and he returned home to pass the time before embarking for Colombo. It was at this stage that he became fascinated by military history. He read detailed accounts of the Boer War, the Russo-Japanese War and the Franco-Prussian War of 1870. He even waded through Clausewitz. He studied comparative religion. He made little headway with poetry, except for Walt Whitman. '*Leaves of Grass* became my bible.'

'Forty-five years later I read in *The Poetry Review* that readers were invited to submit their own recollections of the poem which first appealed to them, in an essay not exceeding two hundred words.' He submitted the following essay and received a complimentary broadsheet and a polite letter.

I received no encouragement to read poetry at home. During my early schooldays, being quite incapable of memorising verse, a punishable failure, I bore all poetry an unremitting grudge. Then, after leaving school, I discovered Walt Whitman. I was overwhelmed. Here, just round the corner, were to be found the answers to all the problems of the Universe, and the purpose of man. Here was practical proof that secrets, untellable in prose, could be revealed in poetry. 'The words of my book nothing, the drift everything.' Impossible of attainment as Whitman's magnificent claims were, his assertion that 'no poem or the least part of a poem but has reference to the soul', seemed demonstrably true. But my continuing though unsuccessful desire to express myself through the medium of poetry came to me one night in the trenches of the First Great War when I read that most tender of all Walt Whitman's poems, 'Reconciliation'. Here is the poem which I still think is one of the most beautiful in the English language:

> Word over all, beautiful as the sky,
> Beautiful that war and all its deeds of courage must in
>   time be utterly lost,
> That the hands of the sisters Death and Night
>   incessantly softly wash again and ever again this
>   soil'd world;
> For my enemy is dead, a man divine as myself is dead,
> I look where he lies white-faced and still in the coffin –
>   I draw near,
> I bend down and touch lightly with my lips the white
>   face in the coffin.

These words were to have an uncanny echo during the action in which he won his Victoria Cross.

Thus, Charles Hudson, aged 19, was his own person, clearly not a run-of-the-mill 19-year-old of the English country gentry at the beginning of the twentieth century.

TWO

• • • • • • •

Ceylon

Hudson was in love when he left for Ceylon. Much later he expressed his feelings in a poem. It is not clear whether the object of his affections did in fact die, or whether this was poetic licence, but there is beauty in these lines.

Lament

I saw her walking on the strand
Where we were wont to walk before she died,
And whispered low 'Tis I, Tis I.'
In vain I sought her midst the mounds of sand
Where we were wont to rest, where first I cried,
'Your lover ever true am I.'

I heard her lost voice singing in the glade
Where we were wont to stroll in summer's heat,
But scarce I dared to breathe 'Tis I.'
In vain I sought her in that sylvan shade
That used to be the place where we would meet
And whisper each 'Your lover I.'

> I feel the gentle kiss of her warm lips
> On mine, in daylit dreams, but dare not wake
> To whisper low 'Tis I, Tis I.'
> I pray to join her as the red sun dips
> Below this empty world, our tryst to make,
> And whisper low, 'My love, tis I.'

Hudson was also very sorry to leave his sister, with whom he had a very strong and lasting relationship. As was the custom in those days she was left to look after her mother. As he put it: 'Not an entrancing outlook.' As we shall see, Hudson was to write to Dolly regularly from the trenches.

He had doubts about his new career.

> Over all there was the haunting fear that I had done a foolish thing in agreeing to busy myself in what I considered would be an entirely uncultured, almost uncivilised, environment with little prospect of escape should I find life as a planter totally uncongenial and pointless. This may sound intellectually snobbish but in my adolescent state of development I was, with very little to warrant it, inclined that way.
>
> My mind was seething with a hotchpotch of undigested ideals centred upon a vague idea that I should devote my energies towards improving the world! Incidentally, the socialists seemed to me to be the only section of the political community who had in their minds any real desire to put right the glaring injustices of our social system. Planting in Ceylon did not seem to present much prospect of achievement. I was in fact a very ordinary unfledged and rather difficult adolescent of my class and upbringing and the proper place for me was a university where I could have let off steam and found my level. Not that this for a moment occurred to me at the time, for financial considerations and the fact that I could not hope to gain admittance by examination into a university ruled out any such thought.

He must have matured a great deal in Ceylon where he went as a 'creeper', the Ceylon colloquialism for an apprentice in the planting world. He was not used to drinking vast quantities of alcohol, indeed he actively disliked it, and he was astonished by the sexual behaviour of the planters who, it was explained to him, automatically took several Ceylonese mistresses spawning innumerable children in the process. He made some friends on the ship who tried to persuade him to accompany them into the brothels of Marseilles and were affronted by what they saw as his extraordinary and rather stuffy refusal. Hudson felt most embarrassed by his apparent lack of 'manliness'.

He had been employed by two brothers 'Bois' for a private experiment of their own – the planting of rubber, a crop which was flourishing in the East Indies and Malaya, but was not yet established in Ceylon.

His local boss was to be a jovial Scotsman, Gavin by name, about 40 years old with a short temper. His wife was a good deal younger, an Australian, good-looking and efficient. They had no children, much to their disappointment. They were both very kind to their new and very naïve creeper. Eventually there were three creepers whose job it was to oversee the labour force which consisted of about 500 Tamils from South India, including women and children, and a number of Sinhalese people who did the more skilled jobs, including blasting, culvert building and tree-felling, by contract with the local Sinhalese village headman. The Tamils were Hindus and the Sinhalese were Buddhists, both with their very different customs, superstitions and religious practices. At that time the Tamils were virtually slaves. They were recruited in South India and lent their passage money by their employer, which they were meant to repay by their labour, but their pay was so low that they rarely succeeded.

In fact, of course, the great majority of European managers were humane men, but there are exceptions to every rule and in the event the coolies had little chance of redress if they were badly treated.

During and after the 1914 war the debt system was done away with. As time went on, companies were forced to provide amenities, such as hospitals, schools and better accommodation, which even the best of them had never before considered their responsibility.

The Bois brothers had bought a large block of land near the sea about 50 miles from Colombo (rubber was only cultivable on the low-lying fringes of Ceylon). Gavin had built a bungalow there and was to open up and plant a series of 300-acre blocks with a system of managers to supervise each block. One new block was already planted. Another was in the process of being felled, roaded and drained.

A second creeper, five years older than Hudson and far more worldly wise, joined soon after Hudson's arrival and lived with the Gavins, as did Charles. They were a happy family. The third creeper had a bungalow of his own where he lived with his young wife.

Mrs Gavin and Hudson started to treat sick Tamils in the evening – an entirely new experience for him as they tried to 'extract long worms from horrible lumps on their legs by winding them out on matchsticks!'

Hudson was in charge of the morning muster and on one occasion was nearly killed when, not realising the Tamil custom of prohibiting any man, including a woman's husband, going into close contact with a female during her menstrual period, he had ordered a gang of women in that condition to go to work with the men. He was attacked by three men, one of whom raised his heavy hoe. He thought his last hour had come. He was only saved by the fortuitous approach of his 'horse keeper'.

As a result of Hudson's actions the whole Tamil force had stopped work and were holding a meeting of protest. It was an extremely difficult situation for Gavin. He was told that a man who had inadvertently defiled himself could only be purged in the eyes of his people by a ceremony that included bathing in water in which a certain ingredient had been dissolved. Hudson agreed to do this but never discovered what the 'ingredient' was. The Tamils were too embarrassed to tell him.

Hudson joined the Ceylon Mounted Rifles. There were six young Europeans in the district and they were able to form an independent section. He bought an Australian Waler, a small chestnut gelding, a comfortable ride but inclined to bolt if suddenly frightened. He went out on exercises with his companions, again feeling highly embarrassed when refusing to join them in their vast and apparently unending bouts of hard drinking. He had to escape through a tent flap on one occasion when his sin of emptying a glass of whisky into a tree tub was observed and he was threatened with running the gauntlet (the offender would be stripped of his trousers and forced to run between two long ranks of troopers with swagger canes, ending with a ducking in a horse trough).

Hudson had other adventures, being charged by a buffalo while shooting snipe and, stupidly, trying to slap a rogue elephant on the bottom with his hand when it was turned away from him in order, he thought, to emulate Gavin who had apparently achieved this feat when much younger. Again, he was lucky to survive.

Perhaps the most shattering event in his stay in Ceylon occurred on his estate.

The latex tapped from our older rubber trees was brought into the Estate factory and there rolled in rollers operated by bands of leather which reached up to the roof. One day a coolie (the common and not derogatory word for a Tamil worker) was caught by the arm, flung up to the roof and killed.

All the Tamil coolies attributed this to the presence of a devil in the machinery and refused to stay on the Estate until the devil had been exorcised. This ceremony could only be carried out by certain Hindu priests, and work stopped until they could be brought over from South India.

We were asked to attend the ceremony during which certain omens would determine whether or not the devil could be driven out. The first part of the ceremony consisted of the slaying of nine goats. Each had to be decapitated in one clean stroke. To effect this, it was necessary for the wretched animal to have its neck stretched out and forward. Failure was a bad omen, and might mean that we would lose our whole Tamil coolie force for good.

The first eight goats were induced to assume the correct position by being confronted by another goat nose to nose. One was held back just out of reach and as the selected animal stretched his neck forward the priest struck. It was a gruesome and gory sight for, as the head was severed a stream of blood spouted from the neck before the body fell.

In the light of flares the circle of men round the executioner chanted a weird song, led by the High Priest, and the women, in their most gaudy sarongs, in a wide circle, clapped in unison.

All went well until the ninth and last goat was dragged forward. Again and again it flatly refused to extend its neck and again and again the burly axe-man, naked except for a loincloth, lowered his heavy axe.

The crowd was tense, and the chanting increased in volume. Groans and moans broke out each time the axe-man paused. At last the climax came, but the head was not completely severed.

A conference of priests was held. . . . The High Priest informed Gavin that in spite of the bad omen the situation might still be saved if a considerable further contribution was made to the priests who in continuing the ceremony were running serious personal risks.

After a show of bargaining and bluster, Gavin had to give in and promised the money asked for.

The next stage of the proceedings was at least less gory. In the centre of the circle a large earthenware jar was placed over the flames of a very quickly kindled fire. The four priests began slowly dancing round the fire to the accompaniment of the tom-toms. The coolie men circled in the reverse direction to the priests while the Chief Priest chanted in a high voice. It was explained that only if the oil came to the boil could the ceremony be continued. If it failed to boil all would be lost. Gradually the rhythm of the drums was speeded up. The dancers became more and more frenzied. The High Priest's voice became louder and louder and more and more high-pitched. As coolies in the circle fell exhausted others leaped in to take their place but still the oil refused to boil. . . . The climax came when a naked Tamil, whom I recognised as the Estate watchman, was seized and pushed into the inner circle. As the four priests gripped him, the Chief Priest shouted that the oil had boiled, lifted the jar and threw the whole contents over the watchman's naked body.

There could hardly have been a more dramatic denouement. With yells of agony the watchman broke his way through the circle pursued by the priests and all the coolie men. In a few moments the whole lot, spectators and all, had disappeared in full cry after the watchman.

Gavin and Hudson were extremely upset. However, it was explained that the watchman had volunteered for the role he was to play, and the devil had been induced by the chief priest to enter his body. When they caught him up the priest would beat him, but only the devil would feel the punishment. This would be so severe that he would fly away.

Thankful that the loss of our labour force had been averted, Gavin had to accept this and agree to pay for a great feast which would be held in celebration of the devil's defeat into the bargain. It is hardly necessary to say that the watchman reappeared quite recovered in a week's time and became the hero of the coolie lines. He was certainly a brave man.

During his time in Ceylon the young Hudson had many other adventures of a similar nature occasioned by the deep superstitions and beliefs of both the Hindu Tamils and the Buddhist Sinhalese.

On one occasion with Richard, a fellow creeper, Hudson found himself in the middle of a furious and dangerous row between Tamils and Sinhalese. It appeared that about twenty Tamils had gone to a Sinhalese village to have a drink. A quarrel had arisen and the Sinhalese had beaten up the Tamils badly. Only one had escaped to tell the tale and the others were apparently wounded or killed or held as hostages in the village. Hudson and his friend clearly had to try to sort things out before worse befell them.

Gavin had always impressed on me that for one or two white men to go armed amongst a number of frightened and angry natives only invited trouble. The threat of force, unless it was really overwhelming force, was worse than useless. An attitude of complete confidence and calmness was above all required. If any weapon was called for, the best of all was ridicule.

I decided [Hudson had clearly become the leader] to take four Tamils to carry lanterns and had great difficulty in persuading them to come unarmed which was not surprising in the circumstances, but I had to take them, as I was not at all sure of the way through the jungle to the village.

We had not gone far when a party of about a dozen Sinhalese armed with long spears fashioned from staves with knives lashed to their ends, leapt out from the jungle shadows across our path. The two Tamils ahead of us cried out for mercy, the two behind fled without further ado. I was ready for something of the sort to happen and I laughed loudly.

'Look at all these brave men so well armed to fight two unarmed white men and two Tamils they pretend to despise,' I called out to Richard. Then, as I flashed my torch round the circle they lowered their weapons and looked, as I had hoped, distinctly sheepish.

The atmosphere changed and they were led into the village courtyard. Hudson told the headman that he must produce at least ten carts to carry the injured Tamils back to their lines.

Villagers were filtering back into the courtyard. The wounded Tamils were beginning to curse the Sinhalese now that they felt safer. The Sinhalese were cursing back. Pandemonium broke loose. On top of all this a bloodstained figure leapt from the ground in front of me and I caught the glint of a knife in the flame of the torch held by the Headman. The wounded Tamil had meant to strike the torchbearer but as I raised my arm to hold him back, the knife, missing the torchbearer, sheared through the fleshy part of my arm just below the elbow. The torch had gone out and Richard and I found ourselves striking out blindly in our efforts to keep our feet in a turmoil of yelling natives.

Eventually order was restored and the Tamils were taken to their lines. Hudson and Richard found themselves trying to deal with the wounded.

Neither Richard nor I had ever set a broken limb. At one o'clock in the morning we set about the job, one of us sawing off and splitting into halves suitable lengths of thick bamboo, the other fitting, as best he could, the broken limbs into these improvised splints. As to the head wounds, we cleaned them up as best we knew how and, pressing the lips of the wounds together as tight as we could, tied bandages clumsily around.

As a 20-year-old, Hudson was clearly learning fast.

As regards the different religions, attempts were made by some Christian missionaries to convert both communities but these were, on the whole, unsuccessful. Hudson got to know one Buddhist monk, a 'dear old man' quite well. He asked the monk if he really believed in some of the more extravagant practices in which the Sinhalese villagers indulged. The monk laughed and said that the Buddhist religion was a very deep philosophy. The poor ignorant peasants could not be expected to understand the higher sacred teachings and, meanwhile, much was countenanced which was not true Buddhism, as long as it did no harm. He was well aware that he himself would have to return to earth many times before his goal was reached. The peasants would need to be reborn many, many times and with each rebirth would learn a greater wisdom.

'I have read your Bible,' he said. 'Do you approve of the bloodthirsty ways of the people of the Old Testament? They too were ignorant men who had to be reborn. . . .' I could only argue that reincarnation was not the only possible solution, as he assumed.

'Oh,' he said, 'You mean they might have gone to Hell forever?' He was a very gentle old man and as near my idea of a saint as any man I had come across before. He was a great admirer of the teaching of Christ, which, he sadly remarked, had been so woefully misunderstood.

'Was it really true,' he asked, 'That there were Christian priests who taught the people that they were eating real flesh and drinking real blood, when in one of the Christian rites they were given bread and wine?' The old man was so distressed and shocked at the thought of this that I tried to deny it, but he said a villager had shown him a pamphlet written by a Christian missionary which distinctly gave that terrible impression.

It was a wiser, vastly more experienced and more tolerant young man who returned to England with his fellow creeper to fight for his country at the outbreak of the First World War.

'Our leave taking of the Gavins was sad,' he wrote, 'for we had become very much a family party. Little did we know that, of the four of us, the two who went to the war would survive and the two who remained in Ceylon would lose their lives in tragic circumstances.'

Mrs Gavin was shot and killed by a resentful Sinhalese servant who had been reprimanded and had been drinking and working up his resentment. Gavin was drowned after the war. He became entangled in some fishermen's nets while bathing and called for help, but the others did not realise until too late that he was not fooling. Charles wrote of Gavin: 'I owed him more than I could ever hope to repay.'

THREE

• • • • • • • • • • • •

War

Why was it that, without question, like many of their ilk elsewhere, Hudson and his companions returned to England to fight for their country? There was no difficulty about leaving his job. The Bois brothers let Hudson break his five-year contract without demur. Indeed, Kitchener's call to arms had an almost embarrassingly immediate, universal and full response. There was great enthusiasm in Britain for the war. Professor Anthony Fletcher of the University of London in the *Journal of the Historical Association* (October 2005) summed it up succinctly:

> The springs of patriotism lay in a Victorian notion of manhood, which was developed in the writings notably of Rudyard Kipling and others. Young men were able to see the war as a Great Adventure. The relationship between paternalism and deference, it is argued, is the key to understanding how the British war effort was managed. Comradeship, achieved through shared suffering, defined men as heroes through their willingness to endure.

The public school system with its cult of athleticism and development of the ability to lead undoubtedly had contributed

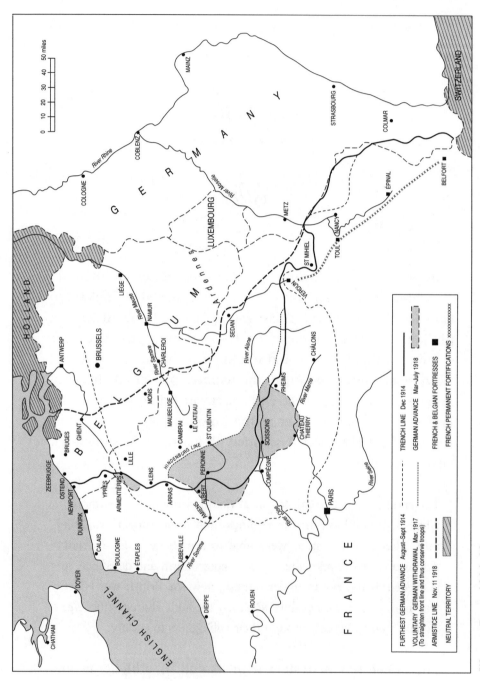

Western Front, 1914–18.

to the remarkable establishment of the British Empire. There was a vast pride in this achievement, which permeated all classes of the nation. British was best – and that was that.

Some opposition to the war remained, but Lloyd George's total support of British action in a speech at the Queen's Hall on the 19 September 1914 was important in this context, as he had passionately opposed British involvement in the Boer War. His peroration was remarkable:

> May I tell you in a simple parable what I think this war is doing for us? I know a valley in North Wales between the mountains and the sea. It is a beautiful valley, snug, comfortable, sheltered by the mountains from all the bitter blasts. But it is very enervating, and I remember how the boys were in the habit of climbing the hill above the village to have a glimpse of the great mountains in the distance, and to be stimulated and freshened by the breezes which came from the hilltops and by the great spectacle of their grandeur. We have been living in a sheltered valley for generations. We have been too comfortable and too indulgent, many, perhaps, too selfish, and the stern hand of fate has scourged us to an elevation where we can see the great everlasting things that matter for a nation – the great peaks we had forgotten, of Honour, Duty, Patriotism and, clad in glittering white, the great pinnacle of Sacrifice pointed like a rugged finger to Heaven. We shall descend into the valleys again, but as long as the men and women of this generation last, they will carry in their hearts the image of those great mountain peaks whose foundations are not shaken, though Europe rock and sway in the convulsions of a great war.

Oratory indeed in our sound-bite age. Earlier in the speech Lloyd George had said:

> I envy you young people your opportunity. They have put up the age limit for the Army, but I am sorry to say I have marched a good many years even beyond that. It is a great opportunity that

comes only once in many centuries to the children of men. For most generations sacrifice comes in drab and weariness of spirit. It comes to you today and comes to us all, in the form of the glow and thrill of a great movement for liberty.

There was a rush to the recruiting offices immediately after this speech. Rapturous acclaim came from all sides including the Conservative Opposition. As John Grigg says in his biography of Lloyd George, however, such sentiments would have come better from the Prime Minister had he not written to his wife a week after the war began:

They are pressing the Territorials to volunteer for the war. [Gwilym] mustn't do that just yet. We are keeping the sea for France – that ought to suffice her for the moment especially as we are sending 100,000 men to help her to bear the first brunt of the attack. That's all that counts – for Russia will come in soon. I am dead against carrying on a war of conquest to crush Germany for the benefit of Russia. Beat the German Junker but no war on the German people and I am not going to sacrifice my nice boy for that purpose. You must write Wil telling him he must on no account be bullied into volunteering abroad.

(*John Grigg*, Lloyd George from Peace to War 1912–1916)

As far as the *casus belli* was concerned, for Hudson this was a simple matter. Germany had invaded Belgium with whom we had a treaty and there was nothing else we could do with honour but come to her aid.

He became very angry when, after the Second World War, it was suggested to him that there was no *casus belli* in 1914 to rival that of 1939. 'In one case Germany attacked Belgium. In the other Germany attacked Poland. We had treaties with both – what is the difference?'

On his return to England Hudson must have been influenced by the massive current propaganda about the German behaviour in Belgium, some of which was undoubtedly true. For example, a Dutchman, Raemaeker, produced some very startling cartoons which were published in England in twenty-six fortnightly parts (*Land and Water*, Empire House, Kingsway, London). These were accompanied by articles often detailing German atrocities by such prominent intellectuals as G.K. Chesterton, Hilaire Belloc, the Dean of St Paul's and others.

Patriotism, pure and unadulterated, was exemplified in the Raemaeker cartoon (page 42): 'My son go and fight for your Motherland.' It was accompanied by a poem by Eden Phillpotts which ended:

> England's your mother!
> When the race is run
> And you are called to leave your life and die,
> Small matter what is lost, so this be won:
> An after-glow of blessed memory?
> Gracious and pure, In witness sure
> 'England was this man's
> Mother: he, her son.'

The first bound volume of the cartoons included 'An Appreciation from the Prime Minister, H.H. Asquith', in glowing terms.

The Germans were seen as arrogant, acquisitive and barbaric. Stories of their atrocities in Britain were lapped up by a public ready to believe in almost any crimes committed by their enemy.

Having undergone a year's training at Sandhurst it was not difficult for Hudson to be commissioned in the Army. The only problem was which regiment he would join. This was easily solved by his mother writing to an old brother officer of his father's, then serving in the War Office. Her letter led to a meeting at the gentleman's office where, to Hudson's horror, he was told that his brother Tommy had been captured and made a prisoner of war. Hudson's sister-in-law Phyllis was not as upset

"TO YOUR HEALTH, CIVILISATION!"

THROWN TO THE SWINE

The Martyred Nurse.

" My son, go and fight for your Motherland ! "

as she might have been since, like everyone else at that time, she expected the war to be over by Christmas. Kitchener's demand for volunteers with the ominous words 'For three years or the duration' had not yet sunk into the national consciousness. Hudson was told that there would be little difficulty in his replacing his brother in his regiment, The Sherwood Foresters, and he returned home to await developments. One fine morning he was bicycling along a straight road when to his horror he heard a band appearing. It was his future regiment on the line of march and he had to stand, wearing civilian clothes, as the whole regiment passed, many of them making ribald remarks about his civilian status, with jeers and catcalls adding to his mortification.

Hudson joined his regiment, the 11th Sherwood Foresters, shortly afterwards and found himself in command of a platoon of about thirty men. They were all volunteers and almost all miners with that mixture of camaraderie and experience of danger typical of those of that particular calling at the time. They were part of the new Kitchener's Army and had joined together when they heard the call to arms, as did no less than 1,186,357 others from August to December 1914.

The training they underwent was, to say the least, of little relevance to the horrors they were to experience. They had no rifles and carried wooden dummies of approximately the same size and shape. At first they had no uniform but wore armbands over their civilian clothes. Eventually rifles appeared and they were allowed to start firing them on the range. As far as tactical training was concerned, there was virtually none. There are distinct parallels to the experiences of the early Home Guard or Dad's Army in 1940.

Attempts were made to practise 'attack', 'defence' and 'withdrawal', but nobody knew what to do and the result was almost total boredom. To add to these miseries, Hudson caught mumps and was absent when the battalion moved to Aldershot where they remained until August 1915 when they went to

France. During their time at Aldershot Hudson's mettle was tested by his platoon. At the end of a night exercise, before returning to barracks, he gave the order to his platoon to 'slope arms'. 'It was still barely light but as the order was completed I could see, quite clearly outlined against the sky, the dead bodies of two rabbits gently swinging from the top of two rifles in the rear rank. I had no idea what to do about it but to gain time I gave the command 'Order arms'. There was some tittering in the ranks and Hudson's platoon sergeant, too, could hardly keep a straight face. Hudson had the two offenders marched in front of the platoon and gave them an almighty rocket and, to his relief, he managed to restore the order which was on the point of collapse. There were other incidents of a similar nature but, he heard afterwards, he had gained the respect of his platoon.

Hudson had been having recurring attacks of malaria, which culminated in his catching cerebral spinal meningitis. It nearly killed him. At one stage he was in an isolation hospital in which forty-eight out of fifty patients succumbed. He was conscious enough to hear his regimental doctor ask a specialist if he thought another lumbar puncture was advisable and heard the answer: 'Better leave the poor chap alone. He won't live until the morning anyway.' Hudson's response was to be furious at the callous way in which 'he seemed to dismiss me' and he determined to survive, if only to spite him.

As the time approached for the battalion to go abroad there was much speculation among the officers as to who would be picked to go. Hudson was told that he would go as second in command of a company – a step up in the military hierarchy. In the event, to his dismay, he was told that the brigadier had asked for him to be his galloper – a sort of additional ADC with the prime task of taking messages on horseback to the battalions under command of the brigade.

The crossing to France was uneventful and the battalion began its slow and long march up to the front. Much to Hudson's sorrow, the brigadier, 'a charming, conscientious, honourable and patriotic man in the highest sense of those terms whom I regarded with considerable awe as a grandfatherly personage' was sent home as being too old and out of date for active warfare. Hudson accompanied him in a sad series of official farewells to his battalions, riding away from each parade in tears. As Hudson put it, 'I am sure that . . . he allowed his imagination to present a picture of himself actually heading the brigade, pistol in hand, in some desperate encounter.'

A new brigadier arrived and Hudson was sent with a message for a battalion. He was trying to conceal one of his malarial bugs at the time, but had a blackout and fell from his horse. He woke up in a military hospital at Bailleul, a converted convent. For the first time he made contact with the horrors of war.

It was a lovely warm summer's day. Suddenly a commotion seemed to break out. A fleet of ambulances had arrived unexpectedly. Stretchers filled with groaning, coughing soldiery were being laid out in the courtyard below me. Many were retching and trying to struggle off their stretchers in spite of the efforts of orderlies to prevent them. These men were gas casualties from a gas attack which had caught our troops without adequate anti-gas protection. The first use of gas on the Western Front had taken place on 22 April 1915. It was now September, but our gas bags, as they literally were, were of little practical use and were often either misused or put on too late.

Because his malaria was not immediately treatable, Hudson found out that he was on a list of those to be sent home. He got out of bed at night, dressed as best he could, crept downstairs and eventually, after an unfortunate encounter with his night orderly, got out of the hospital into the pouring rain without any shoes. He took refuge in the officers' club of the town where the night watchman apparently was not particularly surprised at the appearance of a semi-dressed, shoeless officer, assuming that the earlier part of the night had been spent in a house of ill repute.

When Hudson rejoined his brigade headquarters the brigade major and brigadier had already been informed of his ill-disciplined behaviour but, after a few anxious moments, the Brigadier agreed to overlook his disregard of military law. To his surprised delight he was allowed to return to his battalion in time for its first appearance in the trenches in a quiet part of the line near Armentières so they could get used to trench routine without the shock of heavy casualties.

Hudson was second in command of a company, which was led by a Captain Russell whom he admired immensely. They had been warned not to take unnecessary risks by looking over the parapet in daylight and when, at the dawn stand-to, Russell stood up on the fire step and looked over, Hudson remonstrated with him. 'He had just said "Do you think a sniper could see to aim in this thick mist?" when a bullet shattered the field glasses he was using and blew out the back of his head. I was literally sick with horror and grief. It was our first fatal casualty and the whole company was terribly upset and shaken.'

Charles wrote a letter to his sister headed 'The Trenches, October 1915'.

My dear Dolly,

It is devilish cold at 3.30 a.m. in the trenches. I am on duty from 2 to 5 this morning and am supposed to be patrolling the trenches, but have taken an interval to write in the officers' mess. A temporary affair, 3 sides sandbags and canvas, top corrugated iron and sandbags.

Yesterday we had a bad shock. Poor old Russell, I don't think you know much of him, was killed. He was an awfully good fellow was Russ, real stolid stuff. I don't mean he was a rough diamond, for he was a gentleman by birth as well as by nature. I had been showing him where I had patrolled the night before in front. Then I went to my dugout and he went to fetch some field glasses – he was using them over the parapet foolishly. He had hardly been up 10 seconds before a bullet went straight through the glasses, knocking the back of his head out. He was dead when I got to him and in fact never spoke, poor boy. It makes my heart ache to think of his poor mother. I know he was so fond of her and, except for her, a woman hater by nature.

I have to take over the Company, it is a great responsibility. There I am with 200 men immediately under me. Times are bound to come where one feels incapable of facing it and would like to consult an older head or simply obey. One will feel, I know, 'Have I done everything to safeguard accidents if an attack comes' etc. etc. All that part is the gloomy side, it remains that I have a Company and with the responsibility goes the opportunity. I am the youngest Company Commander by 7 or 8 years!

Today we go into a Rest Camp some miles from here. It will be a pleasant change, although I should like a few more nights here as I have a job to finish. Last night I and a Sergeant (an ex-Metropolitan Police Force man) went out to the German lines. We crawled out slowly, listening, and got right up to the German parapet and reconnoitred their wire. Apparently they are starting a most elaborate system of wire defence. The part we were opposite was completed and I was dying to go tonight and find out details and especially how far the new system went and if they were working on it now.

I would have gone last night, only a damned ass of a Sergeant has apparently gone off his head and went wandering out this morning without leave. When he came in I blew him up and in the afternoon he calmly sent a message to his platoon officer to say he was going and went at about 3 p.m. and hasn't been seen since, it is now 4.30 a.m. I couldn't very well go out when he was about as I don't want to get shot by my own man by mistake and he would probably shoot at sight.

I must go.
Bye-bye
Yours
Charles

Shortly after he had taken over command of the company, Hudson had another horrific experience.

I was sitting in my company headquarters, a corrugated-iron topped shelter cut into the sandbagged parapet, when heavy shelling was concentrated on the remains of a derelict building incorporated in our company sector. One of my platoon commanders, a lad of about 19, was with me. Odd shells were bursting in our vicinity, and the platoon commander, obviously hoping I would advise against it, said, 'I suppose I ought to go to my platoon.'

This was the first time of many that I had to face the unpleasant responsibility of telling a subordinate to expose himself to a very obvious odds-on chance of being killed. I told him he ought to join his platoon. He had no sooner gone than I heard that haunting long drawn-out cry 'stretcher-bearers', to which the men in the trenches were so addicted.

I followed him out, glad of the spur to action. It is so easy to find sound reasons for keeping undercover in unpleasant circumstances. Three company stretcher-bearers were hurrying down the trench. Stretcher-bearers were wonderful people. Ours had been the bandsmen of earlier training days. They were always called to the most dangerous places, where casualties had already taken place, yet there were always men ready to volunteer for the job, at any rate in the early days of the war. The men were not bloodthirsty. Stretcher-bearers were unarmed and though they were not required to do manual labour or sentry-go, this I am sure was not the over-riding reason for their readiness to volunteer.

I had not yet learned that a few casualties always seemed to magnify themselves to at least three times the number they really are and I was filled with horror when I reached the derelict house. A shelter had received a direct hit. I found the subaltern unhurt and frantically engaged in trying to dig out the occupants. The shells were bursting all round the area as I approached, and men cowering undercover were shouting at me to join them. Dust from the shattered brickwork and torn sandbags was flying and this, and the unpleasant evil-smelling fumes from the shells made it difficult to realise what was going on. A man close by me was hit and I began to tend him as a stretcher-bearer came to help me. More shells burst almost on top of us. I noticed how white the men were, and I wondered if I was as white as they were.

Their evident fear strengthened my own nerves. We had been lectured on trench warfare, and it suddenly and forcibly struck me that this bombardment might well be a preliminary to a trench raid. At any moment the shelling might lift and almost simultaneously we might find enemy infantry on top of us. I shouted for the subaltern.

'Were any sentries on the lookout?' I demanded. I stormed at the men and drove the sentries back on to the parapet. The reserve ammunition had been hit and I cursed the subaltern for not having done anything about replenishment. After this outburst, and in a calmer state of mind, I went from post to post warning the men to be on the lookout. Gradually the shellfire slackened and finally ceased.

That night I found myself physically and mentally exhausted. I determined at least not to try and overcome fear with whisky. I wondered too whether the soldiers, when they had recovered, would regard me as having been 'windy'. The word was much used by those who had been at the front some time and, like all soldiers' slang, it caught on very quickly with the newcomers.

Once damned with 'windiness', an officer lost much of the respect of the men and with it his power of control. Had I in fact been unnecessarily windy? I knew in my heart of hearts that I had, though I found out later that my behaviour had not given that impression. It is comparatively easy for an officer to control himself because he has more to occupy his mind than the men. I resolved in future to think more and talk (or shout) less in an emergency.

Throughout the war I never ceased to have, in the back of my mind, the appalling sight of the ghastly wound which I had helped to dress in this first experience of heavy shelling, and I resolved in future that I would never look at wounds, or dead men, if I could possibly avoid it. I had been 'bloodied' as had the company.

On another occasion a subaltern of his was due to go up with a wiring party to do repair work in no man's land.

He was a lusty raw-boned lad, unlikely one would think to suffer from nerves, or a mental breakdown. He had been quiet of late, but I had not realised that his nerves were unusually affected. We were very short of officers, and in any case to send an officer from another platoon was unfair and might do irreparable damage to his own prestige in the company. I reasoned with him and persuaded him to go. He was killed. The men said he had refused to lie down when machine gun fire swept across no man's land, as the rest of the party had quite rightly done. Fire at night was un-aimed and of no particular danger or significance. The men thought him foolhardy. I wondered if he had been paralysed by his own fear, or so afraid of being afraid that he had refused to allow himself to take cover.

Hudson summed up the atmosphere in a letter to his sister on 23 September 1915:

My dear old girl,

Send me writing paper if isn't on its way, and refills for 'Tommy's Cooker' [a solid paraffin contrivance for boiling water etc.]. I'm afraid my demands are numerous but deal with one shop and it is easy.

We spend a lot of our time in bomb-proofs when the enemy are expected to shell, where we are now. They don't seem to have much in the way of munitions now; we did a 30 mins intense this morning just before dawn. It was a wonderful sight, the great flashes of the guns lit up the sky for miles. I stood with my back to the parapet and could see beautifully – most awe-inspiring. They were bursting the German wire and parapet on either side of us and the shells went whiz – louder and louder then bang until the earth shook. Poor Germans! They have to take it lying down now apparently. One battery tried to fight back but our guns for miles turned streams of shell onto them. I could hear them go out towards it like angry bees, fierce as anything, until the battery stopped, which it did pretty quick. They are getting a few more in now but it is absolutely safe unless they get a direct hit – a small risk for war.

It's a marvellous thing, this modern war, and makes one feel pretty small. I wouldn't have missed it for anything, although at times one would give one's soul for it to stop.

Hudson's battalion did not take an active part in the battle of Loos of 25 September 1915 in which the British for the first time made a real effort to break through the German lines. The plan was for Hudson's battalion to advance if the attack was a success and the enemy withdrew. In the event the battle was a costly and complete failure and there was no call for exploitation of success.

Before the battle started Hudson, for the first of many subsequent occasions, saw the effect of a complete loss of nerve by an officer.

On the evening before the attack, company commanders were called to HQ for a final briefing. After the colonel had outlined the plan, the senior company commander, an ex-regular, a horsy type, tall, slim, good-looking and stupid, rose to speak. He pointed out that in accordance with previous orders he had sent out patrols to see if the bombardment had succeeded in cutting the enemy wire. The wire, he said, had not been cut and the other company commanders, including myself, confirmed this. The colonel pointed out that as we would not be asked to advance unless the enemy withdrew, too much importance need not be placed on this. This remark was the occasion for an hysterical outburst from the senior company commander. We were being asked, he said, to sacrifice ourselves against uncut wire. The order amounted to murder, he for one would absolutely refuse to let his men advance against uncut wire. The colonel repeated that our orders were dependent on the success of the main attack and the withdrawal of the enemy, but the Major had completely lost control of himself. In a wild welter of words, he inveighed against our commanders and staffs and their whole attitude towards the fighting troops. How were the staff to know whether or not the enemy opposite our sector had withdrawn? We would be ordered to advance just the same whether they had or not. At this, the colonel broke up the meeting and the Major, I am glad to say, was ordered to hand over his company.

The major was later sent home and disappeared overboard while crossing the Channel – probably suicide, although this was not certain. After the battle had died down the battalion was sent to the Ypres salient where they spent eight months during the winter and spring of 1915/16 until they took part in their first full-scale offensive on the Somme in July 1916.

The conditions in the winter in Ypres salient were appalling. The water was too close to the surface to allow of deep trenches being dug, and this difficulty had been overcome to some extent by the building of ramparts of sandbags above ground level. The cold was intense but frost at least had the advantage of preventing one sinking as deeply into the mud at the bottom of the trench, as was normally the case. As time went slowly on, conditions improved with the increased production of trench boards and the issue of rubber thigh boots. Short rubber boots were a menace as they were always soaking wet. Amenities began to appear in the form of hot food containers, braziers and leather jerkins but only the young and strong could stand up to the conditions for long. Curiously enough my malaria had entirely left me and in spite of being cold and wet for days and nights on end I never had a day's sickness necessitating my being off duty throughout the rest of the war.

I am sure now that I did not appreciate the physical strain on men older than myself, nor did I allow for, or really sufficiently appreciate, the strain and anxiety of the married men. A sergeant in a confidential moment in a long night watch, once said to me, 'It's all very well for you, you are unmarried and haven't a wife and children to worry about, but if I am killed what, I wonder, will happen to my family? My wife is not the managing sort, she has always depended entirely on me, and she has never been strong. Her people are dead and my mother is an invalid herself.' After this I always tried surreptitiously to avoid sending married men on the more dangerous duties, but a high proportion of men, and nearly all the NCOs, were married.

Domestic anxiety was particularly acute amongst a considerable section of men who did not or could not trust their wives. As is well known now to everyone, but was not so well known to me then, relations or friends always get some obscure kick out of warning absent husbands that their wives are 'carrying on'. This type of thing was not by any means confined to the ranks. I had the greatest admiration for a certain RAMC colonel. Few of his rank visited companies in the front line, but he came round frequently, talked to the men, and really knew the conditions under which they lived. He was the commander of the Field Ambulance which normally dealt with our casualties and his visits were very much appreciated. I had been told that he had an appalling temper and treated his own officers very harshly, but he could not have been more charming to me. One day we read in the papers that he had been arrested for murder. When on leave he had shot his wife's lover whom he had found 'in flagrante delicto'. There was much talk in the company of a petition to be sent home from them on his behalf, but nothing came of this as, in fact, he was found to be mad and sent to Broadmoor. Later a lance corporal in my company, whom I knew from the censoring of his letters home had an unfaithful wife, was due for home leave. I had a talk with him, but the only result was that he refused to go home at all. The days of organised welfare had not yet begun.

Records that I still have show that we went out to France with twenty-eight officers and that in ten months twenty-six new officers had been posted to us. Many of the newly joined officers became casualties. The colonel, adjutant and second in command remained and about one officer per company. Not all the officers who had gone had been wounded or killed, many had gone sick, others were just too old or too nervous to stand up to the strain of the trenches. At 24 I found myself well up to, if not above, the average age of the officers.

No man's land in the salient varied from a few yards, incredible as this sounds, to about a hundred yards. Shelling was not as common in the front line itself as further back owing to the proximity of the enemy. Trench mortar fire and rifle grenades were our bugbears in the front line. I preferred, of the two, shelling. A shell came quickly, a trench mortar rose high into the air and then on reaching the apex of its flight came down, turning over and over like an old boot, landing with a thud before it burst. From the apex downwards it always appeared to be making straight for you if you watched it, much as the eyes of a portrait seem to follow the viewer round a room. I learned not to look.

I realise now that my addiction to patrolling was a form of escapism. Like golf in peacetime, being entirely engrossed in the immediate necessity of the moment, the cares and troubles of normal life ceased to be. The physical discomfort of crawling about in wet grass and mud in the cold, without prospect of a bath ahead, were compensated for by the feeling that one was doing something really active which might prove to be of real importance. The thrill and excitement were of the same nature as that experienced by a child playing hide and seek after dark at home, but on patrol one was both the hunted and the hunter. Not that a kill was the end in view for information was wanted, and this entailed the avoidance of any bloodthirsty encounter. I usually carried a revolver as a matter of form, but it was a nuisance and I was very tempted to leave it behind. A good strong pair of wire cutters was more important. I always carried a few selected stones in my pocket, with which to distract the attention of an inquisitive sentry. A bomb would wake everyone up, a stone judiciously lobbed would distract him enough to allow time to get out of an awkward position while the sentry was peering in the wrong direction.

I never took more than one companion on patrol. One of these was an ex-Metropolitan policeman, an Army sergeant. He often regaled me with stories of the suffragettes during the heyday of their aggressiveness before the war. The police had much to put up with, but even when the suffragettes took to stabbing them with hatpins they kept their temper. But a limit was reached when a party of leading suffragettes was arrested and taken to a police station. They should have been put in cells for the night, but out of kindness of heart the police gave them the use of their own private billiard room, provided a meal from their own canteen, and beds, blankets and sheets. In the morning the women were found to have deliberately cut and torn the billiard table to shreds.

My other patrolling companion, also a sergeant, but later promoted to commissioned rank, had been in peacetime an agitator in a mining area. He was one of the best, the firmest and most humane disciplinarians I have ever met. I was very fond of both these men. They were quiet and dignified, utterly loyal and trustworthy, and both had a nice sense of humour. If they thought I was being unduly reckless they would warn me, but would follow me without further question if I insisted. Knowing this, I hesitated before I asked them to do anything I knew they would regard as foolhardy, for they were both married men.

Though I must have gone out on patrol hundreds of times, I never once fired a shot, and only once had shots deliberately aimed at me.

On one occasion he found a chink in a sandbagged wall deep in German territory:

Peeping through this I found myself looking into a dugout. The door into the trench was open and an NCO was, I supposed, calling the next sentry for duty. . . . The men in the dugout lit a candle as the door closed and in its light I could see the men opposite me quite distinctly. Three sat in a row on a bench. I had never seen the enemy, other than prisoners, at a range of a few feet and I was vastly intrigued. Then a man just the other side of the wall shifted his position so that the back of his neck blocked my view. I blew gently and the man scratched his neck but did not move.

Hudson wrote again to his sister:

BEF, France
1915

My dear Dolly,

I feel most fearfully gloomy, my heart being somewhere in my boots, though I daren't show it.

We came out of the trenches the other day with hardly a scratch. Yesterday I went to lunch with HQs. I am living now with my own Coy again (last time in billets with HQ). Suddenly we heard a crash just short of the farmhouse, out everybody dashes for cover in trenches near. Just as I reached the outer door another crash on the road, the next thing – 6 men on the ground. One, Captain Brennan, in the ditch, but he was all right, only shaking and mumbling. The doctor was just behind. We got them all into the cellar, but two whom we couldn't help, one my

Coy, a signaller, the other a sergeant of B Coy (next for leave) poor chap. Two more will die, in fact they were dying in the cellar but were sent on the ambulance which arrived later. Poor Brennan has gone back for a bit to the Transport (he will be in the paper 'suffering from shock'). I hope he will be all right, we can't afford to lose any officers. Poor lad I was sorry for him, every nerve straining for the next. These billets are damnable. However, having got this off my chest I must forget and grin and turn the gramophone on. I bought a gramophone when on leave, all in five minutes, but it is a good one and the records they sent are good too.

While in the trenches I did another crawl and have been thanked personally by the General! Swank. I have got a letter too, thanking me for the report and saying it has been forwarded as before to Div HQ.

I await events and will forward results as before for the collection!

You may be pleased to hear I was absolutely forbidden by the General to go again as I am a Coy Commander, rather rot for me but –

I went with Stafford again, at 4.30 a.m.

Conversation: 'Damned cold Sergeant.'

'Yes Sir, moon's a bit bright, but it will be going down soon.'

'Yes Sir, better take some bombs.'

'Yes Sir, shall I get them Sir?'

'We'll pick them up at the listening post (in front) sentries warned?'

'Yes Sir.' So off we go through a covered gap in the parapet and down the ledge.

'Who's that?' (whispered).

'Sherwood Foresters Captain Hudson.'

'All quiet Corporal?'

'Yes Sir.'

'We're going out in front to the left.'

'Very well Sir.'

We are now 150yd from Fritz and the moon is bright, so we bend and walk quietly onto the road running diagonally across the front into the Bosche line. There is a stream the far side of this – boards have been put across it at intervals but must have fallen in – about 20yd down we can cross. We stop and listen – swish – and down we plop (for a flare lights everything up) it goes out with a hiss and over the board we trundle on hands and knees. Still.

Apparently no one has seen so we proceed to crawl through a line of 'French' wire. Now for 100yd dead flat weed-land with here and there a shell hole or old webbing equipment lying in little heaps! These we avoid. This means a slow, slow crawl head down, propelling ourselves by toes and forearm, body and legs flat on the ground, like a snake.

A working party of Huns are in their lair. We can just see dark shadows and hear the Sergeant, who is sitting down. He's got a bad cold! We must wait a bit, the moon's getting low but it's too bright now 5 a.m. They will stop soon and if we go on we may meet a covering party lying low. 5.10. 5.15. 5.25. 5.30. And the moon's gone.

'Got the bombs, Sergeant?'

'No, Sir, I forgot them!'

'Huns' and the last crawl starts.

The Bosch is moving and we crawl quickly on to the wire – past two huge shell holes to the first row. A potent row of standards are the first with a nut at the top and strand upon strand of barbed wire. The nut holds the two iron pieces at the top and the ends are driven into the ground 3ft apart. Evidently this line is made behind the parapet and brought out, the legs of the standard falling together. All the joins where the strands cross are neatly done with a separate piece of plain wire. Out comes the wire cutter. I hold the strands to prevent them jumping apart when cut and Stafford cuts. Twenty-five strands are cut and the standard pulled out. Two or three tins are cut off as we go. (These tins are hung on to give warning and one must beware of them.) Next a space 4ft then low wire entanglements as we cut on through to a line of iron spikes and thick, heavy barbed wire.

The standard has three furls to hold the wire up and strive as we can, it won't come out. 'By Jove, it's a corkscrew, twist it round' and then, wonder of wonders, up it goes and out it comes! It is getting light, a long streak has already appeared and so we just make a line of 'knife rests' (wire on wooden X—X) against the German parapet and proceed to return. I take the corkscrew and Stafford the iron double standard. My corkscrew keeps on catching and Stafford has to extract me twice from the wire, his standard is smooth and only 3ft so he travels lighter. He leads back down a bit of ditch. Suddenly a sentry fires 2 shots which spit on the ground a few yards in front. We lie absolutely flat, scarcely daring to breathe – has he seen? Then we go on with our trophies, the ditch gets a little deeper, giving cover! My heart is beating nineteen to the dozen – will it mean a machine gun? Stafford is gaining and leads by 10yd. 'My God,' I think, 'it is a listening post ahead and this the ditch to it. I must stop him.' I whisper, 'Stafford, Stafford' and feel I am shouting. He stops, thinking I have got it. 'Do you think it's a listening post? There! By the mound – listen.'

'Perhaps we had better cut across to the left Sir.'

'Very well.' This time I lead. Thank God, the ditch and road over the ditch, and we run like hell-bent double. Suddenly I go a fearful cropper and a machine gun is rattling in the distance and the streak is getting bigger every minute.

'Are you all right Sir?' from Stafford.

I laugh, 'Forgot that damned wire.' (Our own wire outside our listening post). The LP occupants have gone in. Soon we are behind the friendly parapet and it is day. We are ourselves again, but there's a subtle cord between us, stronger than barbed wire, that will take a lot of cutting. Twenty to seven, 2 hrs 10 minutes of life – war at its best. But shelling, no, that's death at its worst. And I can't go again, it's a vice. Immediately after I swear I'll never do it again, the next night I find myself aching after 'No Man's Land'.

Some yarn I think, worse than the Wide World, tell me if it sounds realistic, it's all the truth.

Don't you wish you were here. I'd give anything for peace. I heard from Phyl tonight, she says poor Tommy is getting more and more depressed, poor lad.

My nerve has quite come back again. I felt a bit shaky when I started. I got a good letter from you, old girl. Give my love to Miss Fitzherbert. I am sure she wants a man to make her live, as I want a woman! Work out her own career indeed! I didn't dislike JP a bit, I merely wasn't impressed, but often the people unimpressive at first are the nicest after. He seemed nervous and there were always others to draw my attention.

Bye-bye
Ever your loving Brother
Charlie

PS I have two samples of wire still and will send them if I can think of a method – giving contents is difficult. The standards etc have gone with the report. Isn't it rotten the corkscrews are just beginning to be used by us – a demonstration of their use was given the day I brought one in.

They had not been in Belgium for long, but long enough to be deeply insulted when a scheme was initiated for the amalgamation of Regular with Kitchener Army battalions during tours in the front line.

My company was to combine with a company of the Lincolns. The Lincoln company commander was to take over my company sergeant major and second-in-command and I his. Platoons were similarly intermingled. This scheme was so unpopular that it was abandoned after each of the mixed companies had done one tour in the trenches. I took a mixed company in first and all went reasonably well but on the second night of the Lincoln company commander's tour he sent for me to go up to the line. On arrival I found that my company sergeant major, whom he had taken over, was drunk. He had withdrawn into a trench shelter where he sat with a German revolver threatening to shoot anybody other than his own company commander, myself, attempting to interfere with him.

Hudson went up to the front line and put him under arrest. It turned out that in Hudson's company the rum ration was always under the control of an officer (the company sergeant major's proclivities being known). In the Lincolns, however, no distinction had been made between an officer and a senior warrant officer. The strain had been too much. He was court-martialled and reduced to sergeant.

So what kind of youth was Charles Hudson, having just had his 24th birthday, as he prepared for the massive test of character and nerve that he was to face at the Battle of the Somme in charge of some 200 men? He certainly had no illusions about his chances of survival without either death or a 'blighty' wound – the latter meaning the bliss of a comparatively light wound just enough to warrant evacuation home. Fear was ever present. As he put it:

There is a saying that war consists of 90 per cent of intense boredom and 10 per cent of intense fear. This is the sort of generalisation that men liked to quote in their more supercilious moments in the comfort of peacetime after the war. As regards the actual front-line troops of the 1914 war it was entirely untrue, though there was some truth in it for the mass of the Army, who very rarely got near enough to the front line to come under fire.

For us, boredom was entirely the wrong word. One could hate the life but one could hardly be bored by it; fear was ever with us.

Apart from this, the criticism of our commanders who were always driving us to further endeavour and the responsibility towards our juniors who were always needing attention and thought and, above all, the heaviness of spirit caused by the loss of friends, oppressed us. As time wore on, I found myself shying away from becoming too intimate with newcomers for fear of the added pain and emptiness which would follow should they be killed or wounded. As for physical fear, there were of course the more intense times but always at the back of the mind was the obvious statistical fact that few, very few, infantry front line officers survived the trenches for more than a few months. It was possible to push fear into the back of the mind during some spells of short home leave or behind the line in training, as came our way, but hardly possible to avoid the fear that a return to the danger area would mean a wound or death.

He must have been a difficult subordinate, disobeying orders when he felt like it. His obsession with patrolling no man's land at night was eventually in direct contradiction to orders, and we shall see later many examples of this trait. The only mitigating factor was that his disregarding of orders was always the result of his wishing to undertake some offensive action and never to avoid danger or undue exertion.

Clearly, due to his experiences, mature beyond his years in many ways, he retained a boyish enthusiasm and almost childlike delight in the hide-and-seek game in the dark which he described with such relish. He was, at times, absurdly foolhardy – blowing into the crack in the German dugout. He acknowledges the fact that it was much easier for officers to keep their nerve, with responsibility for others to think about, than it was for the soldiers under them who could only think of themselves. As we have seen, there were many officers who lost their nerve. Hudson did not scorn these people, but felt desperately sorry for them and tried to help – a hopeless task when someone had really cracked up.

His emotional attitude to war was very mixed. Against a background of constant apprehension about the immediate future, at times his spirits were lifted. He even went so far as to use the words already quoted (page 51) in a letter to his sister that he wouldn't have missed it for anything. He added, however, that at the time he would give his soul for it to stop. There is an astonishing paradox in the fact that many people can only feel truly alive in the face of death when all the humdrum inanities of 'normal' existence are banished. This may explain the lure of rock-climbing, mountaineering and other extreme sports.

Hudson remained throughout the war an essentially serious person, writing to his sister about the many books he was reading. As we have seen, he knew precisely why his country was at war with Germany.

As the war went on, there were of course many people who thought Britain ought to make peace with Germany, particularly after the horrors of the trenches became more apparent. This belief had been fully documented. To cite just one example, in a vivid and passionately angry poem, Wilfred Owen put into words what many thought. In the poem 'Dulce et Decorum Est' the last words read:

> If in some smothering dreams you too could pace
> Behind the wagon that we flung him in,
> And watch the white eyes writhing in his face,
> His hanging face, like a devil's sick of sin;
> If you could hear, at every jolt, the blood
> Come gargling from the froth-corrupted lungs,
> Obscene as cancer, bitter as the cud
> Of vile, incurable sores on innocent tongues –
> My friend, you would not tell with such high zest
> To children ardent for some desperate glory,
> The old Lie: *Dulce et decorum est*
> *Pro patria mori.*

Hudson took a different view. He wrote from Italy to his sister in
March 1918:

> Your account of the Labour Reunion makes me furious. If I
> could ever make a good speech it would be on the subject of
> peace or war at this moment. It makes me sick to think of the
> swine who sit at home and, knowing nothing of any emotion,
> except those affecting their fat stomachs, talk of making
> overtures to the people who have for years laid themselves out to
> crush every instinct of a decent minded gentleman, and in the
> attempt have killed and maimed thousands of those fat bellied,
> grovelling swindlers' own kith and kin.
>
> If they had seen a trench, as I have, so filled to the top with
> dead and dying, in their agonies, and the look of terror on brave
> men's faces and all the horrors of a war, they couldn't sit calmly
> in their seats and listen to proposals for climbing down to those
> who made such things possible. I haven't got time to write a
> speech but I wish to God people at home would try to realise for
> one moment what realities are before they start into talk. I would
> rather die a thousand times than let these poor boys suffer what
> so many have, for nothing.

Although, like everyone else in the trenches, he greatly
looked forward to the occasional leave, he found the total
ignorance at home of what was actually happening at the
front very upsetting. On one occasion, having left the squalor
and horror of the trenches with mangled bodies, blood and
mud a central feature of existence, he went to stay with his
mother in Sussex and was asked to a tea party by the local
vicar whose wife greeted him, 'Ah, Mr Hudson, you are one
of our brave boys from the front. Now would you like a
cucumber sandwich or perhaps a piece of cake? Or both?
And I know that Gwendolyn would love to play tennis with
you – but have your sandwich first.' The contrast was almost
obscene.

Later, he wrote,

My mother now lived in a flat in London, and owing to my long absence in Ceylon before the war, and my continued presence with my regiment since my return, I knew no one of my own age to consort with in England except my sister who herself was much tied with her own war work. She was worried with my obvious inability to amuse myself or be amused. In spirit I was a million miles from normal life and could only try to fill the void by a continuous round of theatres and music halls and foul-aired restaurants. What I wanted was peace, the country and a congenial company, but the practical difficulties were great, nor did I myself realise the need at the time.

Leaves, nevertheless, in that they meant freedom from fear, were a heaven sent relief and the dreary return journeys to France were a misery. I hated that dreadful returning leave train from Waterloo Station to such an extent that for years after the war I had a recurrent nightmare of arriving late, missing the train, and being in the shadow of a court-martial for cowardice. In my nightmare, in spite of frantic efforts to get to the station, I was prevented, I lost my way, I lost my ticket or my luggage, I got embroiled with sinister and shadowy thugs, and commonest of all, I was in a huge hotel at night and could not find the room where all my belongings were.

On two occasions, when on leave, he suddenly burst into uncontrollable tears in a taxi, to the astonishment of both the taxi driver and himself. He had never broken down in the trenches or when in reserve but once right out of the atmosphere of war the tensions became uncontrollable in him. On the other hand, apparently on one occasion, later, he was offered a choice between a recommendation for a third DSO or a week's leave. Unhesitatingly he took the latter.

One day in the trenches, when the German trenches were only about a 100yd away, he was himself in a front-line trench when he turned round and, to his great surprise, saw the Prince of Wales standing behind him. With great charm the Prince apologised for being a nuisance but asked if he could use a periscope which his mother had given him to look over the top of the trench in the hope of seeing a real live German. He was in the act of lifting the large and rather unwieldy instrument so that he could see over the top when a posse of extremely worried staff officers rushed up, seized the periscope from the Prince and admonished him for, as they saw it, his foolhardy actions. 'Sorry,' said the Prince to Hudson, 'I hoped I had given them the slip,' and, with a rueful look, he was escorted away.

FOUR

· · · · · · · · · ·

The Somme

Death

Why did you pass me by, why?
We've often met before, you and I
Familiar on the field of war.
It's true we've often met before
When bullets whistling, crack,
And shells following their track,
Whining their way, burst,
Messengers that thirst
For blood. While pitter, pat, pat, pat,
Debris comes tumbling down, and masonry
Crashes in doom and the boom, boom, boom,
Of friendly canon fire, and musketry
And automatic guns whose rat-tat, rat-tat,
Perform the cruel symphony of war,
Exciting me, confusing all my wit.
While wounded retch and curse and groan and spit
And groan, and groan and groan in choral misery.
Why did you pass me by?
We've met in hospitals before

In peaceful times, in times of war.
The last a tented hostelry
Where Army Sisters softly tread
Twixt row and row and row of stretchered bed
And fear in all its devilry
Repeats itself as patients shout
Delirious. When dead are carried out
By orderlies, deep in the shadowed night,
In rubbered shoes, midst men who in their dreams
Fight on, seeing disaster in the beams
A gentle moon has cast in silvered light
Why did you pass me by, Ah why?

The 11th Sherwood Foresters arrived in the Somme area in March 1916. Initially the area was comparatively quiet. Hudson still continued with his night patrolling in spite of direct orders to the contrary. However, with full official support for a change, he organised a raid on the German trenches in order to capture some prisoners. He and the ex-agitator sergeant examined the German trenches opposite his sector of the front line, at night, in great detail.

All seemed now set for the perfect trench raid. With the aid of air photos a model was constructed and parties trained in their respective duties. A 'box barrage' would fall round the dugout area, the back of which would consist of a rain of shells on the enemy's second line; the sides of the box were to cut across the enemy front line, well clear of the dugout. Our plan was to capture the occupants of the dugout. The enemy front line within the small area to be isolated by fire would receive no shells, as the plan was to hide men under the cover of the enemy parapet itself. Their special duty would be to leap into the trench and surprise the sentries at the same time as another party rushed through the narrow entrance to capture the occupants of the dugout. The leader of each party I took out personally and showed him exactly what to do on the ground. We even arranged to lay a telephone to the trench entrance, and for stretchers to be in position under the enemy parapet.

On the night of the raid the assembly went perfectly to plan. I was with the gunner observation officer in our own front line, and this was cleared of men to avoid the inevitable counter shelling. We hoped that the raiders, with their prisoners, would be back so quickly that they would be clear of our front line before the enemy had had time to appreciate what had happened and call for counter artillery fire. Never, I thought, had a raid been so well laid on. I could think of nothing that could go wrong when the whole raiding party was safely in position and through the enemy wire.

The gunner, myself, two telephonists and my orderly waited tensely. The gunner was counting the seconds to zero hour. It seemed an age but exactly at zero the dead silence of the night was shattered by a whirlwind of projectiles and ear-splitting crashes.

The shells seemed to be skimming just over our heads and bursting almost in our faces.

'Aren't they a bit close?' I shouted above the din. In the flashes of the bursts I could see the gunner's face. He looked aghast.

'They're short,' he yelled back, 'Shall I stop them?'

'No,' I said, 'Tell them to lengthen the range.'

In desperation he yelled, 'I can't now, it's too late. I can only tell them to stop.'

It was a dreadful moment. Just when all seemed to have worked out so perfectly, more perfectly than I had dared hope, to stop it now! But there was no alternative; there was no possible doubt, something had gone wrong, and our men were being fired on by our own artillery, who were bursting their shells on the enemy front line instead of their second line. Shouting to the gunner officer to stop the fire, I ran down the trench to the exit from our line. Already odd men were struggling back. I brushed by them and out into no man's land. Suddenly, as if by magic, the shelling stopped. In the darkness I blundered almost on top of a stretcher party.

'Who is it?' I whispered.

'It's the officer, Sir,' a voice a replied.

We had lost a first-class officer, and a few, mercifully and surprisingly few, men were wounded. They were all picked men and the best I had. Weeks of planning and preparation had been wasted, the men's faith in their supporting artillery and myself had been badly shaken, casualties had been caused, and all to no purpose. It was a bitter blow and hard to bear. The gunners had misunderstood the plan and had assumed they were to fire on the enemy front line. The fact that the gunner battery commander was sent home was little consolation.

The battalion had a new Church of England chaplain.

He was an incredibly simple soul, completely out of his depth. Though about 28 he had no idea of what are normally called the facts of life and confided in me that he was often very embarrassed by the men who, discovering this, used to pull his leg. Poor chap he was terribly serious-minded and was worried to death because his nerve had failed him, and he attributed this to lack of faith. I was very sorry for him. The culmination came when he was conducting a burial. He had just committed the body to the grave when the enemy started shelling. In a panic he followed the corpse into the cover of the grave.

Apparently his robes acted as a kind of parachute as he descended. He then had to climb out in the face of the burial party who looked totally bemused and astonished. The shame and horror of this episode so preyed on his mind that he had to be sent home.

Hudson spoke of a character

for whom my admiration was unbounded, and in whom I put complete trust. He was a private soldier and my servant and his name was Gibbs. A railway man in peacetime, married, with a young family. A man of peace by nature and quite incapable of appreciating the first principles of a military outlook on life and behaviour. He was a good deal older than myself and well above the average age of the early Kitchener Army men. There was no reason why he should have volunteered to join when he did. He made no claim to heroism or to any highfalutin' sense of duty, he just joined up because many of his friends had, and he was not going to let them join and stay behind himself. He always kept his clothing and equipment clean, but he was quite unable to look the part of a soldier, or to behave smartly on parade, and he was very conscious of his inability to do so. I was careful not to favour him in any way by excusing him from formal appearances on parades, and it always amused me to note how successive sergeant majors, fiercely determined to see that no one should evade parade, fell in turn to his attractive simplicity, and soon found themselves almost shamefacedly providing him with exemptions from parade.

'I suppose you will be wanting Gibbs tomorrow morning at such and such a time,' the Serjeant Major would say, hoping to inveigle me into excusing him from parade.

'Oh no, I can perfectly well do without him,' I would reply cheerfully.

Then after the parade I would say to the Serjeant Major, 'By the way, I didn't see Gibbs on parade. What happened to him?'

'Well, Sir, we had to send a reliable man to do such and such, and I thought Gibbs was just the right man to send, you said you would not be requiring him,' the Serjeant Major would say.

Gibbs treated me almost tenderly, as a father might treat a headstrong and rather reprobate son.

'Out again last night,' he would say when he woke me after a night patrol, gazing ruefully at a mud-encrusted uniform, and half sadly, half-humorously, shaking his head as much as to say, no good will come of these nights out. Gibbs and his battered suitcase (my suitcase) solemnly trudging up communication trenches was a well-known figure. It never seemed to occur to anyone else to carry a suitcase into the trenches, nor did it seem to be quite in accordance with military etiquette, but Gibbs would never have thought of that, and his slow, charming and disarming smile would have put any officious person at a complete disadvantage if they had attempted to interfere with him. He could not be hurried; he nearly always avoided marching with the rest of the company in the ordinary way, but he and his suitcase would never fail to turn up. He never shirked taking his fair share in any work that had to be done, however unpleasant. Everybody liked him.

One night in the salient at Ypres a very heavy bombardment of our sector of the trench woke me up. Hurriedly I lit a candle and pulled on my boots. I heard shouting in the trench above, a few steps up, and then the cry of 'gas!' I searched round for my gasbag, and was fumbling under the bunk, when Gibbs appeared and joined in the hunt. I was still poking round the dark recesses of the dugout when I heard Gibbs say, 'There it is, Sir, on the bed.'

Rising from my knees I was just in time to see his legs disappearing up the steps.

I grabbed the satchel and was about to pull out the bag when I saw Gibbs' own number and name on the underside of the flap. I dashed up the steps shouting 'Gibbs!', but he had vanished. The gas attack was in fact a false alarm, but when he left me his own bag and went up, as he thought, to face a ghastly death, he did not know that.

Besides the shelling the enemy were machine-gunning our parapet. The noise was appalling and the men had begun to fire back wildly, as they sometimes were inclined to do when some panicky sentry started them off. It was all I could do to restrain them and it was not for some time that I saw Gibbs again. When I did, he said quite sincerely and calmly, as if his preparedness to sacrifice his life for mine had been the most natural and obvious thing in the world. 'It was much more important that you, as company commander, should have a gas bag than that I should.

As a private soldier I wouldn't have made much difference anyhow if it had been an enemy raid.'

Before our first set-piece battle on the 1 July 1916 on the Somme, I rather shamefacedly gave Gibbs a letter addressed to my mother, 'just in case'. He took it without a word and put it carefully in his tunic pocket. After the battle I never asked for it back and vaguely assumed that he would have destroyed it. Other battles followed but I never took any similar action with regard to them. Then the day came when, as a result of my representations, Gibbs was to leave us. He had had several close calls. The last was when he was sitting with a few companions behind a broken-down billet. A shell hit the wall above their heads and the men were smothered in the falling masonry and rubble. All received varying degrees of injury except Gibbs, who emerged white and shaken. We had been about to move off up to the trenches when the shelling broke out and the men were having their dinner. As we pulled Gibbs out he said, 'Your kit's quite all right, Sir, but they've spoiled my dinner.' Nevertheless this incident finally shattered his nerve, and with tears in his eyes and not far from my own, we parted. Just as he left he pulled an oil-cloth folder out of his tunic pocket and produced my letter, then nearly a year old.

'I thought you might like to have this back,' he said, 'I'm glad I never had to send it.' Then with his charming half smile he added, 'But it wasn't your fault that I didn't have to, all the same.'

I had arranged for him to join a railway unit. He was not much of a correspondent nor, for the matter of that, was I, but I kept sufficiently in touch to meet him again with his family after the war. He was very much the same in the uniform of a railway guard as in that of a soldier. Friendly, humorous, respectful but never subservient. I was furious to hear that not long after he had left me on the Somme, he had been posted to the railways but then he had been sent to act as engine driver to the train which ran night after night into a station siding at Ypres. There he had to remain until the train was unloaded, sometimes for several hours and frequently under shellfire. When I thought of the thousands of railway trained soldiers who were operating in safety well behind the lines, it made me very angry to think that he, of all people, should have been picked on for so dangerous a duty. I wrote in protest, and after a time he was relieved.

The Battle of the Somme was to last from 1 July until 19 November 1916, when the British finally gave up the attack. The battle was largely the result of the French plea to the British to take some action in order to relieve the enormous pressure under which they were coming at Verdun. The new British Commander-in-Chief, General Haig, assembled four armies for this battle. The main effort was to be made by the Fourth Army under General Rawlinson. The 11th Battalion of the Sherwood Foresters was one of four battalions in the 70th Brigade of the 8th Division in this Fourth Army. A reserve Army, under General Gough, mainly consisting of cavalry, was to exploit the expected breakthrough and move into the open country behind. The other two armies were to make diversionary attacks and safeguard the flanks of the Fourth Army as it advanced. The Fourth Army consisted entirely of the county regiments of the British Army except for some Newfoundlanders and the Bermuda Volunteer Rifle Corps. Rawlinson's Fourth Army ration strength was 519,324 men. A battalion, if at full strength, consisted of some 1,200, a company of some 120 men. Although, after the battle, General Haig liked to call it a great success, it was in fact a major disaster. At the end of the first day, the British had lost 21,000 killed and 35,000 wounded – a staggering figure. In comparison, the German losses were insignificant.

In his journal Hudson describes the battle as he saw it.

After the strain of month after month in the Ypres salient, the Somme and the spring weather was almost a picnic throughout

March, April, May and early June. But as time went on the imminence of the great Spring offensive, which was to win the war, hung more and more oppressively over us. It was like waiting for a major surgical operation which was inevitable, but the date of which could not be fixed. Elaborate and very detailed orders for the coming battle came out, and were altered and revised again and again. Inspections and addresses followed each other in rapid succession whenever we came out of the line. The country, miles ahead of our starting trench, was studied on maps and models. Mouquet Farm, the objective of my company on the first day, will always stand out in my memory as a name, though I was never to see it.

Our battalion was to be the last of the four battalions of our Brigade to go 'over the top'. We were to carry immense loads of stores needed by the leading battalion, when the forward enemy trench system was overrun, and dump our loads before we advanced on Mouquet Farm. In the opening phase therefore, we were reduced to the status of pack mules. We flattered ourselves however that we had been specially selected to carry out the more highly skilled and onerous role of open warfare fighting, when the trench system had been overcome.

Never in history, we were told, had so many guns been concentrated on any front. Our batteries had the greatest difficulty in finding gun positions, and millions of shells were dumped at the gun sites. Had all the guns, we were told, been placed on one continuous line, their wheels would have interlocked. Nothing, we were assured, could live to resist our onslaught.

The first unpleasant hitch in the arrangements occurred when the attack was put off for twenty-four hours. It was later postponed another twenty-four hours. The explanation given was that the French were not ready. Our own non-stop night and day bombardment continued. We were in the front line, with the assaulting battalions behind us in reserve trenches. Apart from the strain of waiting, we found our own shelling exhausting, and received a fair amount counter-shelling and mortaring in reply. We remained in the front line from 27 June until the night of 30 June, when we were withdrawn to allow the assaulting units to take up their positions. As a result of the forty-eight hour postponement the men were not as fresh for the attack as we had hoped, and there was a feeling abroad that a lot of ammunition had been expended which might be badly missed later.

That night, 30 June, we spent in dugouts cut into the side of a high bank. Behind us lay the shell-shattered remains of Authuile Wood, and further back the town of Albert. That night I was asked to attend a party given by the officers of another company. Reluctantly I went. Though no one in the smoke-filled dugout when I arrived was drunk, they were far from being sober and obviously strung up. Their efforts to produce a cheerful atmosphere depressed me. Feeling a wet blanket, I slipped away as soon as I decently could. As I walked back, the gaunt misshapen shell-shattered trees looked like grim tortured El Greco-like figures in the moonlight. I tried to shake off emotion, and though feeling impelled to pray, I deliberately refused myself the outlet, for to do so now, merely because I was frightened, seemed both unfair and unreasonable. Fortunately I could always sleep when the opportunity arose, and I slept normally well that night.

Though my company was not due to move up the communication trench until some time after zero hour, breakfasts were over and the men were all standing by before it was light. At dawn the huge, unbelievably huge, crescendo of the opening barrage began. Thousands and thousands of small calibre shells seemed to be whistling close above our heads to burst on the enemy front line. Larger calibre shells whined their way to seek out targets farther back, and shells from the heavies, like rumbling railway trains, could be heard almost rambling along high above us, to land with mighty detonations way back amongst the enemy strong-points and battery areas behind.

It was not long before the electrifying news came down the line that our assault battalions had overrun the enemy front line and had been seen still going strong close up behind the barrage. The men cheered up. The march to Berlin had begun! I was standing on the top of the bank, and at that moment I felt genuinely sorry for the unfortunate German infantry. I could picture in my mind the agony they were undergoing, for I could see the solid line of bursting shells throwing great clouds of earth high into the air. I thought of the horror of being in the midst of that great belt of explosion, where nothing, I thought, could live. The belt was so thick and deep that the wounded would be hit again and again.

Still there was no reply from the enemy. It looked as if our guns had silenced their batteries before they had got a shot off. I climbed down the bank anxious for more news. When our time came to advance we had to file some way along and under the embankment before turning up the communication trench. A company of the support battalion was to precede us and their men were already on the move gaily cracking ribald jokes as they passed by.

They had not long been gone when the enemy guns opened. This in itself was rather startling. How, I wondered, could any guns have survived? Only a few odd shells fell near us but the shelling farther up seemed very heavy. We were not, then, going to have it all our own way. Impatient, I slipped on ahead of the company to the entrance of the communication trench up which we were to go.

Some wounded were already being carried out and I wondered whether the stretchers would delay our advance. As I neared the trench, I saw the Brigade trench mortar officer, and went to get the latest news from him. To my disgust I found he was not only very drunk but in a terrible state of nerves. With tears running down his face, and smelling powerfully of brandy, he begged me not to take my company forward. The whole attack he shouted was a terrible failure, the trench ahead was a shambles, it was murder up there, he was on his way to tell the Brigadier so.

I did my best to get him to control himself, as the men of my company were approaching. I even threatened him with my revolver, and this for a moment quietened him. Then as my leading platoon came up he started shouting again. I hit him as hard as I could and he fell down blubbering. Telling the platoon sergeant to follow on I went ahead and left him. I never saw him again.

The drunken mortar officer had been right. As we neared the front line, the trench became practically jammed with the wounded and dead of the support battalion who had passed us so short a time ago. The shelling was intermittent but very accurate. I could not, in my worst dreams, have imagined anything more ghastly. It was practically impossible to move forward in the narrow trench without treading on dead men and had we tried to bind up the wounded, many of whom were screaming in pain and fear of being wounded again, we should never have got through. The sight of a headless man sitting in a horrible natural position, leaning back against the side of the trench, was too much for a very young orderly I had with me. He became hysterical and started shouting in a high-pitched scream. The platoon sergeant, just behind him, hit the boy hard across the cheek with his open hand, and with a shudder and a look of complete amazement he recovered and regained his control.

'I'm sorry, Sir,' he said to me, 'I'll be all right now.'

Already we were late, and I began to wonder if we would ever get the company through. Our orders were to file along the front line trench, preparatory to our advance, but when at last we reached the front line, I soon realised this plan would be impossible. Machine guns were raking the top of the parapet, and we would just be mown down. I remembered a short piece of trench that ran out through our wire to a listening post. Not far into no man's land from the end of this trench was the bank which my subaltern had thought was occupied by the enemy. I determined to make for this, and from the shelter of the bank to decide on the next step.

We found the short length of trench packed tight with wounded. Some begged for help, some to be left alone to die. I told the company sergeant major [CSM] to set about clearing the trench of wounded while I went to tell platoon commanders the alteration in our plan. When I got back the CSM was bending over a severely wounded young officer. He was very heavy and when an attempt was made to move him the pain was so acute that the men making the attempt drew back aghast. The trench was very narrow and as he lay full-length along it we had to move him. As long as I live I shall not forget the horror of lifting that poor boy. He died, a twitching mass of tautened muscles in our arms as we were carrying him. Even my own men looked at me as if I had been the monster I felt myself to be in attempting to move him. Sick with horror, I drove them on, forcing them to throw the dead bodies out of the trench.

At last the way was clear, and I called up the first platoon to go over the narrow end of the trench, two at a time. I was to go first with my two orderlies, and Bartlett, the officer commanding the first platoon, was to follow. I told the CSM to wait and see the company over but he flatly declined, saying his place was with company HQ and that he was coming with me. I hadn't the heart to refuse him.

As I ran, wisps of dust seemed to be spitting up all round me, and I found myself trying to skip over them. Then it suddenly dawned on me that we were under fire, and the dust was caused by bullets. I saw someone standing up behind the bank ahead waving wildly. He was shouting something. I threw myself down. It was the second-in-command of the support battalion, an ex-regular regimental sergeant major of the Guards and a huge man. He was shouting, 'Keep away, for God's sake, keep away!'

I shouted back, 'What's up?'

'We are under fire here,' he yelled, 'You'll only draw more fire.'

I realised that the fire came not only from in front of us but from across the valley to our left and behind us. My plan was hopeless. The young orderly who had had hysterics was hit. He cried out and was almost immediately hit again. I crept close up against his dead body, wondering if a man's body gave any protection. Would that machine gunner never stop blazing at us? In an extremity of fear I pulled a derelict trench mortar barrel between me and the bullets. Suddenly the fire was switched off to some other target. The CSM had been hit as he had been crawling towards me. I had shouted to him to keep down but he crawled on, his nose close to the ground, his immense behind clearly visible, and a tempting target! It is extraordinary how in action one can be one moment almost gibbering with fright, and the next, when released from immediate physical danger, almost gay. When the CSM let out a loud yell, I shouted, 'Are you hit?'

'Yes, Sir,' he shouted back, 'But not badly.'

'That will teach you to keep your bottom down,' I shouted back, upon which there was a ribald cheer from the men nearby. When I reached the CSM he was quite cheerful and wanted to carry on, but was soon persuaded to return and stop more men leaving the trench.

Bartlett had taken cover in a shell hole and I rolled in to join him as the firing swept over us again. Besides us, the hole was occupied by an elderly private of one of the leading battalions. He was unwounded, quite resigned, and entirely philosophic about the situation. He said no one but a fool would attempt to go forward, as it was obvious that the attack had failed. He pointed out that we were quite safe where we were, and all we had to do was to wait until dark to get back. I asked him what he was doing unwounded in a hole so far behind his battalion. He said he was a regular soldier who had been wounded early in the war, and that he was not going to be wounded again in the sort of fool attacks that the officers sitting in comfortable offices behind the lines planned! (I give of course a paraphrase of his actual discourse.) He said he certainly would not be alive now if he had not had the sense to take cover as soon as possible after going over the top, as he had done at Festubert, Loos, and a series of other battles in which he said he had been engaged. He reckoned that this was the only hope an infantryman had of surviving the war. When the High Command had learned how to conduct a battle which had a reasonable chance of success, he would willingly take part! I told him if he went on in this way, I would put him under arrest for cowardice.

It was a strange interlude in battle, and I realised that my own uncertainty as to what should be done gave rise to it. I was agitated, feeling that inactivity was unforgivable, particularly when the leading battalions must be fighting for their lives, and sorely needing reinforcements. It seemed useless to attempt to get forward from where we were, even if we could collect enough men to make the attempt. In the end I forced myself to get out of the shell hole and walk along parallel with the enemy line and away from the valley on our left, calling on men of all battalions who were scattered about in shell holes, to be ready to advance when I blew my whistle.

This effort, in which I was supported by Bartlett, was short-lived. Bullets were flying all round us both from front and flank. One hit my revolver out of my hand, another drove a hole through my water bottle, and more and more fire was being concentrated upon us. Ignominiously I threw myself down. We were no better off.

It was up to me to make a decision. Bartlett quietly but firmly refused to offer any suggestion. I took the only course that seemed open to me, other than giving in altogether as the defeatist private soldier had so phlegmatically advocated, and I so vehemently condemned. We returned to our own front line, crawling all the way and calling on any men we saw to follow us, though few in fact did.

There was no movement in no man's land, though one apparently cheerful man of my own company, a wag, was crawling forward on all fours, a belt of machine gun ammunition swinging under his stomach, shouting, 'Anyone know the way to Mouquet Farm?'

A soldier I did not know was running back screaming at the top of his voice. He was entirely naked and had presumably gone mad, or perhaps he thought he was so clearly disarmed that he would not be shot at! Bartlett and I reached our trench without mishap and began working down it, trying to collect any men we could. The shelling on the front line trench had stopped. At one trench shelter I came on a sergeant who had once been in my company, and at my summons he lurched to the narrow entrance of the tiny shelter. I thought at first he was drunk.

'Come on, Sergeant,' I said, 'Get your men together and follow me down the trench.'

'I'd like to come with you, Sir,' he said, 'But I can't with this lot.'

'I looked down and saw to my horror that the lower part of his left leg had been practically severed. He was standing on one leg, holding himself upright by gripping the frame of the entrance.

At the junction of the front line with a communication trench further down the line, I found the staff captain (not the one with the broken nerves). I told him I was collecting the remnants of our men, and asked him if he thought I ought to make another effort to advance. I knew in my heart that I only asked because I hoped he would authorise no further effort, but he said that the last message he had had from Brigade HQ was that attempts to break through to the leading battalions must continue to be made at all costs. He told me our colonel and second-in-command had gone over the top to try and carry the men forward, and both had been wounded. I must judge for myself, he said, but there had been no orders to abandon the attack.

I discovered from the staff captain what had happened. The leading battalions had swept over the enemy trenches without opposition, but had not delayed to search the deep dugouts, as this was the job of the supporting battalion. As the supporting battalion had been held up by shellfire, the German machine gunners in the deep dugouts had had time to emerge from their cover and open fire.

It seemed clear that, unpleasant as the prospect was, a further effort to advance must be made. There was a slight depression in no man's land further to the right, which would give a narrow column of men, crawling, cover from fire from both flanks and front. I determined to try this, and the staff captain wished me luck.

Bartlett had by now collected about forty men, and standing on the fire step, I told them what had happened. There could not be many enemy in the front line, I said. If we could once penetrate into the enemy trench it would not be difficult to bomb our way along it; then we could call forward many of our own men who were pinned to the ground in no man's land. I painted a very rosy picture. One more effort and victory was ours. Hundreds of battles had, I said, been lost for the lack of that one last effort.

We had got a good many men over the parapet when a machine gun opened up. I do not think the fire was actually directed at us but I was just giving a man a hand up when a bullet went straight through the lobe of his ear, splashing blood over both of us. The men in the trench below were very shaken, though not more than I was! The man hit wasted no time in diving into cover, but there was nothing I could do except stay where I was, as the men would never have come on if I were to disappear into the cover I was longing to take. Luckily the enemy machine gunner did not swing his gun back as I had feared.

When all the men were over the parapet, Bartlett and I started to crawl past them up to the top of the column. Not a shot was being fired at us and I told Bartlett to pass the men as they came up, down a line parallel to the enemy trench, while I crawled on a bit to see if the wire opposite us was destroyed. I heard a few enemy talking well away to our left, a machine gun opened up, but it was firing away from us. The wire seemed fairly well destroyed. I slipped back to Bartlett to find that only eight men had reached him, and that no one else seemed to be coming. Eight men were enough to surprise and capture the machine gun post, and once taken, we could call up reinforcements from no man's land. It suddenly occurred to me that I had no weapon in my hand except a large pair of wire cutters, but at this moment I heard enemy shouting. Through a gap in the enemy parapet I could see a German running down the trench; no doubt there were others behind him. It was now or never. I jumped up and feeling rather absurdly dramatic, I ran along our short line of men shouting 'Charge!' Bartlett was at my heels and as I turned towards the enemy line some men rose to their feet.

I remember trying to jump some twisted wire, being tripped up and falling headlong into a deep shell hole right on top of a dead man and an astonished corporal. Soon a shower of hand bombs were bursting all round us and the corporal and myself pressed ourselves into the side of the shell hole. When I had recovered my breath I shouted for Bartlett and was relieved to hear a muffled reply from a nearby shell hole.

It was now about eleven o'clock on a very hot day. Bartlett and I managed to dig our way towards each other with bayonets, but we failed to get in touch with any of our men, who had apparently not come as far. The corporal turned out to be badly wounded and in spite of our efforts to help him his pain increased as the day wore on. Whenever we showed any sign of life the enemy lobbed a bomb at us and we soon learned to keep quiet.

That night, except for an occasional flare and a little desultory shelling, was absolutely quiet. In the light of a flare it seemed as if the whole of no man's land was one moving mass of men crawling and dragging themselves or their wounded comrades back to our trenches. Bartlett and I tried to carry the corporal but he was very heavy and in such pain that he begged me to be put down at frequent intervals. There were some stretcher-bearers about and I sent Bartlett to find one but he lost his way and I did not see him again until next day.

In the end I crawled under the corporal and managed to get him onto my shoulders. He died in my arms soon after we reached our own front line.

It seemed to be stupid just to turn myself into one more stretcher-bearer, and resisting the almost overwhelming desire to help the wretched wounded who were crying out all round, I headed back down the trenches to find Brigade HQ. Dead tired and rather dazed as I was, I lost my way in the now almost unrecognisable trenches. At one point I found myself in a deep and little damaged communication trench leading down an abrupt slope. It was pitch dark and I was groping my way long. Then a flare went up and to take advantage of the light I started running. I suppose my nerves were in a bad state, for without warning a wild panic seized me. Dead men's hands seemed to be reaching out for me, trying to hold me back. The faster I ran the more panicky I became. As the light died out I tripped over a dead man and fell heavily. I lay still, telling myself aloud to pull myself together.

At last I found Brigade HQ. A blanket curtained off the HQ dugout, and as I pulled it aside, the glare of an acetylene lamp nearly blinded me. The dugout was stifling hot and through thick tobacco smoke I saw a group of strangers sitting round a table. Then I recognised our Brigadier seated at the end of the table.

'I have come to report, Sir,' I began, but could not think what to report. After stammering more or less meaninglessly about the need for more stretcher-bearers, suddenly the whole horror of the day overcame me and to my shame I burst into tears.

The Brigadier turned to his Brigade Major, 'Take him away,' he said, not unkindly, 'and give him a drink.' Dazed, I was lead away, pushed into a bunk and handed a strong whisky.

The Brigade Major told me the strangers were officers from a relieving battalion. I could not lie there in the dark doing nothing while all those wounded were wanting help, so after a while I got up and re-entered the dugout.

'May I speak, Sir?' I asked. 'I'm quite all right now.'

The Brigadier was annoyed at this second interruption of his conference, but I was not to be put off. Whether it was the whisky or the renewed return to a normal military world I do not know, but by now I felt completely master of myself. I soon found myself appealing direct to the colonel of the battalion who had been sent up to take over the line from us. I told him he had the opportunity of a lifetime. There were, I asserted, very few enemy left in the opposing front line and they must be entirely exhausted. They could have very few bombs or ammunition left as they had been cut off most of the day by our own leading battalions, who had overrun them. Our continued shelling must have totally disorganised the enemy further back. Now, and before they had had time to reorganise, was the time to capture their front line and from there penetrate their rearward trenches.

The colonel said that his men were entirely strange to the sector and that to attempt a night attack in such conditions would be madness. I told him I could guide them into our old front line and that from there they only had to advance straight across no man's land and into the enemy trenches opposite. The wire was reasonably well cut and by, say, three or four o'clock in the morning the enemy would be far too worn out to put up anything of a fight.

What, I asked, was the alternative? To wait until the enemy wire had been repaired and reinforcements had been sent up? Two whole battalions of our men were in behind the enemy; it was unlikely that they had all been killed or captured, many would still be lying about between the lines and the enemy would not risk sending up reinforcements until that situation had been cleared up, which it would be soon if nothing was done. I pointed out that once we were established across no man's land with our left flank resting on the deep valley on the left, the enemy trenches on our right could be turned. On the other hand if nothing was done now, the whole operation would have to start again. Whether these arguments were sound I do not to this day know, but no action was taken, and it was many months before any advance was made, and much blood was shed in the process.

I acted as guide to a company of the relieving battalion and spent what remained of the night in helping with the wounded.

When, as it was getting light, I reached the rendezvous given for the survivors of our battalion, I was thankful to find my horse and groom still awaiting my return, though the groom was just about to give me up for lost. I was utterly exhausted and climbed with difficulty into the saddle.

Out of a battalion strength of 710 men, including the transport men and 10 per cent who had been left out of the battle, we had lost 508 men. Out of twenty-seven officers, twenty-one were killed or wounded. Only one other officer who entered the battle, besides myself and Bartlett, survived unwounded.

Thus, one of the many firsthand accounts of the first day of the Somme. The vast miscalculation about the efficacy of the German dugouts in protecting their occupants from the damage occasioned by the massive British artillery bombardment led to the mass slaughter of thousands of British soldiers. It is astonishing, to say the least, that this colossal defeat seems to have had little effect on the Commander-in-Chief, Haig, who continued to order fresh attacks day after day and, later, month after month, in spite of the clear evidence that ambitious and far-reaching plans for a final break-through would not succeed in the face of tenacious, well organised and – let us say it – brave German resistance based on machine gun and artillery fire, however massive the preliminary bombardment might be. One amazing fact to emerge much later, and confirmed in his diaries, was that Haig himself never actually visited the front line to see the effect of his strategy and tactics on the men he was commanding. He apparently felt that, if he did so, he would be so upset that his judgement would be impaired and that he would be unable to do his duty in continuing to order attacks at whatever cost.

Having been one of the only three officers of his battalion to survive the first day of the Somme unscathed, when a new commanding officer appeared Hudson found himself adjutant. A draft of 500 non-commissioned officers and men appeared with twenty-one officers. They were nearly all from Irish regiments and were wearing their own regimental cap badges when they arrived. When they were marched to the quartermaster's stores to hand their badges in and receive Sherwood Foresters badges, they refused to do so. A compromise was eventually reached whereby they were allowed to keep their badges but actually wore Sherwood Foresters badges. However, the situation became impossible and they were posted away to be replaced from drafts from various English regiments. A short period of training then ensued.

By the end of July, the battalion was back in the battle of the Somme taking over newly won ground from a battalion which had dug itself into large shell holes which were as yet unconnected. The battalions spent the next six days under almost continuous shellfire, trying to connect the shell holes up with each other. It was very hot and there was a great shortage of water. The stench of revoltingly swollen dead bodies was an additional problem. In these six days the battalion suffered 200 killed and wounded other ranks, 3 officers killed and 2 wounded. They were then sent to a quiet sector of the front in Belgium but by 18 September they were back once more on the Somme. Their old colonel and adjutant had returned from England having recovered from their wounds, Hudson returning to command his old company.

The British were still attacking and wresting pathetically small areas of shell-holed ground from the enemy.

This was the war of attrition, by which was meant that if you went on killing the enemy at a slightly faster rate than your own men were killed, you would eventually win the war. We did not of course know at the time how near the French were to surrender, and how necessary it was for the British to draw off any German attack upon them.

Always we hoped that one more effort would see us through the continuous enemy trench system into the open country. Our leaders, for the most part firm adherents of cavalry warfare, held the cavalry corps close behind us, impatiently waiting for an opportunity to break through like a raging torrent. We in the infantry did our best to close our eyes to the fact that wire and machine guns had long outdated horsemen. We still hoped that cavalry would sweep round the strongpoints, cutting them off and leaving them to be dealt with by the slower-moving infantry as they followed up. Ever the chimera of one more push! The few available tanks were not yet sufficiently developed to be mechanically reliable and the generals were probably right in having no confidence in them.

There then occurred a quite extraordinary incident. The 11th Sherwood Foresters were taking over part of the front line near the village of Martinpuich, which was a total ruin. Hudson's company held a block across a short length of trench: the enemy was the other side of it. The rest of his company was disposed in platoon areas in disconnected shell holes. Air photographs showed that the enemy post consisted of a short length of trench joined to a first-class lateral trench known as 26th Avenue, a name well known in British staff circles as a powerful and important objective. Beyond 26th Avenue lay the village of Courcelette – the objective of the Canadian Corps for the next day, although Hudson did not know it at the time. He went up his trench to the block to investigate. 'The enemy were undoubtedly there. We could smell their tobacco quite distinctly.'

With his usual controlled impetuosity, Hudson crawled out and round the block. He found that the enemy post was not protected by barbed wire; 26th Avenue itself, however, was heavily guarded by a thick line of unbroken wire. He determined to attack the enemy post that night, to advance down its short line of trench to 26th Avenue, thus avoiding the barbed wire and then to capture 26th Avenue itself. The enemy would undoubtedly be totally surprised by the attack.

As a tactical principle I was convinced that this method was far better than a frontal attack against machine guns and wire. I had had enough of advancing in straight lines, but I was by no means sure that my superiors had. By the time an artillery barrage had been worked out and our men had been arranged in a suitable formation we would be likely to lose yet another 100 men without having achieved anything. It just was not good enough.

He telephoned the adjutant to ask if he could carry out his plan. The adjutant was reluctant to wake the colonel who was asleep. Hudson said he would await orders but in the meantime would make the necessary preparations which were considerable. The most important aspect of this – apart from making sure that his men had the necessary bombs and other offensive weapons and had completely understood the plan – was to enthuse them with the confidence that the operation would be a success and comparatively casualty free.

Hudson then received a call from his commanding officer who was impressed with his arguments but would not allow the operation to go ahead without permission from brigade. The line to brigade, he said, was out of action but linesmen had gone out. After some argument the colonel said he would ring back at the latest half an hour before the proposed zero hour. No call came.

Although there were many instances during his career of Hudson's disobeying orders, what followed was probably the most flagrant. He went out himself and cut the wire to battalion headquarters. The die was cast.

As the line had 'broken down' I could say that being unable to get direct orders I felt justified in using my own initiative. By zero hour all was ready. The party to rush the block was ready, I was with the subaltern lying in no man's land nearby in order to rush the trench junction on 26th Avenue.

As I saw the bombs at the block rise into the air against the sky behind us and well to our left flank, I gave the order 'Throw!' to our own party. The officer and three men were to throw bombs at the junction before rushing forward. It seemed an age before their bombs exploded; then we rushed.

My plan was that they should make for the unwired communication trench, while I myself would run straight on right up to the wire protecting 26th Avenue and lob one bomb accurately right into the junction at a range of only 5 to 10yd. It would burst before the assault party could reach it. Then I would lie down and throw a few more bombs further along the Avenue trench to prevent any enemy charging our men at the junction as they arrived.

All this went exactly as planned as far as I was concerned. I had thrown my bombs and had run back again. I leaned over the edge of the communication trench into which the subaltern and his men had jumped. Dead silence! What on earth had happened? Had they turned the wrong way and were they heading back into our own block assault party? The fear of a terrible fiasco gripped me. Then as I peered down into the deep communication trench, a hoarse whisper greeted me.

'Come on, Sir. There's no one here, they are on the run!'

By dawn we had occupied about 100yd on either side of the trench junction, had dug one sleepy German out of some odd corner, astonished to find himself a prisoner. We had sent back a few enemy wounded by our bombs. As I entered a deep dugout near the trench junction which had evidently been an HQ a phone rang. I picked up the receiver. An angry German voice was gabbling excitedly into the instrument. I started storming back in as guttural a gibberish as I could muster. There was a sudden silence and then I heard the receiver being slammed down. How I wished I had been able to speak German!

There was no doubt the Germans had bolted. We must have caught them at the very moment when they were about to withdraw, for a candle was still alight on the table, and officers' kit, boxes of rations, soda water bottles and bedding rolls, all packed ready to move, were lying about. Later we found, to our doctor's delight, the whole of a German medical outfit in a dugout further along the trench.

The line to battalion headquarters had been mended and Hudson wrote a short message to be relayed to corps headquarters where it caused a great deal of excitement because the Canadians were to attack Courcelette that morning and at 11 a.m. a corps concentration of heavy gunfire was due to land on 26th Avenue. The barrage was cancelled and Hudson's company stayed where they were.

As was his wont, Hudson did not remain where he was awaiting events to unfold. It was very foggy and he went forward with his orderly. He lost his way and found himself in the middle of a battery of German guns. Realising where he was, he returned to his company and was preparing to attack the guns from their rear and capture the whole outfit, but when he got there the Germans had vanished.

To his total surprise he then heard the sound of trotting horses which turned out to be a small party of Canadian cavalry who were lost and were delighted to be told what the situation was and where their own front line lay. (Many years later, Hudson met a Canadian in a London club who turned out to be one of the Canadian party.)

Hudson's company now watched the Canadian attack on Courcelette from a gallery seat. He was appalled by the 'inferno of bursting shells, flying bricks and dust, in which miniature human figures rushed about like ants in all directions. It was not possible to distinguish to which side they belonged; we could only just thank God we were not in the shelling ourselves and sympathise with those who were, of whatever nationality.' In these words there were intimations of the fellow feelings many of the combatants on both sides felt for each other, caught up in the seemingly endless and pointless almost daily massacres in which they were all, willy-nilly, involved.

The next attack in which Hudson's company was involved came at the end of September. As always, a small proportion of each rank was kept out of battle and Hudson was chosen for this role. He had to watch his company going into action without him – a difficult and tragic situation as he saw it. His second-in-command of whom he was very fond, 'A gentle creature who only asked of life that he should be left in peace on a farm deep in the country', was killed, as were two other officers and twelve other ranks and about the same number wounded.

As far as they were concerned the battle of the Somme was now over and they returned to Ypres, which they reached in November 1916.

The grim prospect of facing another winter in the salient of Ypres was now before us. To the cold and wet, the mortaring and the shelling was now added the fear of underground mines. The conditions in the trenches had been improved by liberal trench boarding, but as drainage in the low-lying ground was practically impossible, flooding was a common experience.

At about this time Hudson was awarded the Military Cross (MC). The ostensible reason for this was the taking of 26th Avenue and it amused him to think that his total and active disregard of orders had resulted in him receiving this award. Before that he had been awarded the French Croix de Guerre. He found this an embarrassing occasion as he seemed to be the only officer from the front who was being awarded this decoration; the rest were all from the staff and were beautifully turned out. Hudson wore a pair of dirty old puttees. He was amused to see the mortification of General Plumer, an officer for whom he had the greatest regard, being highly embarrassed when he was kissed by General Nivelle who was presenting the awards.

The Battle of the Somme brought about a sea change in the attitudes to the conflict of much of the British Army. As Hudson put it:

On the first shattering day of the Somme battle, when 60,000 officers and men had been mown down, the Volunteer Army of Britain had been devastated and much of the comradely volunteers' pride and spirit had gone. From now on the emphasis amongst the majority, both of officers and men, was not 'How can we get into the fighting?' but 'How can we keep out of it?' Nevertheless the morale amongst the troops still remained of a very high standard though of a less aggressive nature. Those who had lost their nerve or who anticipated doing so, were unashamed of finding some means of avoiding the more active forms of service.

For the rest of his life, Hudson remained silent for the whole of 1 July every year. At first he did not explain why, but later his family came to understand the reason and, of course, respected his silence.

In early 1917 Hudson (aged 24) increasingly found himself acting as second-in-command of the battalion. The winter was wet and cold and, although at first the casualties were light, the Ypres salient was, as ever, unrelentingly uncomfortable and unpleasant. The battalion occupied a slight prominence known as Hill 60, which was bisected by a deep railway cutting. The headquarters' dugout was on the side of the cutting below which stairs led deep down into the mineshaft. A maze of tunnels led thence well under the enemy line. A company of Canadian miners lived and worked there trying to outmine the Germans, who were embarked on the same venture.

Tunnelling and counter-tunnelling went on day and night, each side trying to get round or underneath their opponents hoping to blow a small charge to cut them off. The Canadians were supremely confident, some of them remaining underground permanently until relieved. They never wore uniform and all military convention was disregarded, officers and men being unrecognisable and, often, half-naked. They were, however, a very tough and well-disciplined body of men.

It happened that the commanding officer was on leave and Hudson was commanding the battalion when, on 9 April, the enemy mounted a major attack on the Sherwood Foresters' section of the front. For hour after hour shells rained down on their trenches. Occasionally information filtered down to battalion headquarters through breathless white-faced runners. Casualties were mounting. The front line was reported to be unrecognisable and practically all the wire was blown to smithereens. Hudson decided to withdraw from the front trench because by the time the attack came the soldiers there would undoubtedly be too exhausted to resist it. He knew that any request to withdraw from the front line and consolidate on the support line would be refused were he to ask for permission. Typically, he decided not to ask but to carry the plan out without formal permission. The important thing was to hold the entrance to the mineshaft if necessary with the Canadian help. Hudson went to see them.

Most of them were naked to the waist and they took collective and strong objection to being called on to do what they maintained was an infantry job. Moreover, they pointed out that they had very few rifles between them. I told them that the Germans might very well soon blow the mine entrance and that an argument as to whose fault it was would then be of only academic interest. As I left them, pick helves were being issued out, and they were cheerily assuring me that if we would show them where the goddamn Huns were they would soon clear them out.

Meanwhile, a hand bomb fight was going on in the new front line, round one post left in the old front line. The platoon of the reserve company arrived in time to turn the scale in our favour, but they had had to pass through the enemy barrage, and they arrived without an officer or senior non-commissioned officer.

I took the remnants of the reserve company forward, but arrived to find the enemy had already been thrown out, without the help of the Canadians, leaving thirty-one dead behind them, and I was able to report the situation all quiet and our defences intact, though in a parlous state.

Shortly after this action the whole course of his life was settled for him in the most casual way imaginable. A form of application for a regular commission arrived. He had never given the matter of his future any thought beyond vaguely supposing that after the war, should he survive it, he would return to Ceylon. A commission as a second lieutenant in the Regular Army was offered from the date of signing the form. At the time he was a temporary captain and acting major and the prospect of starting again as a second lieutenant did not seem attractive. Laughing, he seized the form, struck out second lieutenant and wrote in captain. He had long forgotten the incident when, as acting commanding officer, he received official notification that His Majesty the King had been pleased to grant his application for a commission in his Regular Army, in the rank of captain!

The next action in which Hudson participated was the full-scale attack on Messines Ridge. Nineteen mines had been laid under the enemy lines, including a monster which was in place opposite the Sherwood Foresters. They were to be set off in person by the Prince of Wales who, on pressing a button, would detonate all the mines in one great explosion. Hudson was acting second-in-command of the battalion and was supposed to remain at battalion headquarters with the colonel. As usual, however, he refused to have a passive role and against the colonel's wishes he went forward with the very young signals officer, Dickie Bird, who was to be his adjutant in Italy.

The attack had been rehearsed in great detail and, among many other matters, the soldiers had been told not to enter the crater formed by the massive mines. However, some did so and were drowned or killed by gas.

When Hudson arrived on the scene, in practice virtually commanding the battalion, the enemy front and support lines had been taken, but

I found amongst our men a spirit of atrophy due to their unimaginative disregard of the dangers ahead. We were on the left of the whole nine miles of attack and at any moment the enemy on our open flank might recover from the shelling they had undergone and launch a counter-attack. The unnatural quiet was ominous, but to the men it was a blessed relief. I knew how they felt; they had accomplished what they had set out to do, having reached their objective. They had enjoyed rounding up prisoners and had felt human in handing out cigarettes in exchange for souvenirs, a button or a badge or a pay book, which would one day be proudly displayed to admiring girls at home; but I was not the less angry with them.

Hudson stormed about urging the officers and men to immediate action in creating a defensive position. At one point an enemy attack did come in and Hudson, with some other soldiers, found himself cut off. He got hold of a rifle grenade and fired it to land behind the enemy bombing party.

I saw to my amazement that bombs were now being thrown in the reverse direction, away from us. There was soon no doubt that two enemy parties were bombing each other. The grenade must have dropped between them, and each party, supposing they were being attacked, began throwing in reply. So as a result of a pure fluke the counter-attack against us died out. We never learned what casualties the enemy had inflicted on themselves.

The battle continued. Various alarms succeeded each other during the rest of the day and night but the Sherwood Foresters held their ground. They lost 43 killed and 175 wounded. Messines was proclaimed a brilliant success. Though he did not know it at the time, Hudson was put in for a Distinguished Service Order (DSO), which in due course he received.

The battalion was then moved north.

For a month we were living like sewer rats in the squalor of mud and blood officially described at the battle of Paschendaele (or the third battle of Ypres). Trench maps of the area were crystal clear, enemy strongpoints were shown and named . . . all were well-known names at the time. Trenches were lettered and numbered in careful sequences and plans of attack were drawn up on paper and carried out in practice, though the action of the troops on the ground bore little relation to the plans, for the ground consisted of just one featureless mass of waterlogged shell holes. By day the men lay about in misery unable to move or dig themselves in. At night no one dared to move, except along trench boarded routes, for fear of getting drowned, or stuck firmly in the glutinous mud. It was only just possible to exist; reliefs were extraordinarily difficult to effect, and sometimes they entirely failed because the relieving unit could not find those they were to replace.

The generals in command continued to order attacks.

Each time a barrage had been worked out and ammunition laboriously brought up, the infantry detailed for the attack rose obediently from such cover as they had been able to secure for themselves and plodded forward a few hundred yards to occupy the shell holes or remnants of trench that the Germans had vacated. . . . When the attacking troops were too exhausted to struggle on or were heavily machine-gunned they would report 'Objective taken'. Occasionally intelligence officers in higher HQ would query too outrageous a claim, but as a rule the maps would be complacently marked up, whether the claim corresponded with the facts or not.

By this time Hudson was official second-in-command of the battalion. His memory of that month was just a blur of floundering about in the mud searching for companies in the dark; of shelling and being shelled.

There were, however, a few incidents which stand out in my mind like peaks protruding through the clouds. One was of our American doctor, imperturbably attending to the wounded during a burst of shelling, his only protection a few sheets of corrugated iron and some waterproof sheets.

The USA had only recently become our active allies. As a token of the future, America had sent some doctors to France and one, Bayne Jones [*author's note* – eventually he became godfather to the author of this book and a distinguished member of the medical faculty of Yale University] had joined us. Quiet, modest, almost shy but with a strong character, a charming personality and a deep sense of duty, he more than anyone else I had met in the war stood out both as a man and as a doctor. Being an American, he was different, but his quiet presence made us all, officers and men, want to show the best that was in us. He, too, had the greatest admiration for our soldiers and the way they accepted their hard lot even when wounded. It was easy to attribute this to their lack of imagination, but he recognised something more than this in their fortitude, and was unstinting in his praise.

Perhaps my most vivid memory of Paschendaele was one early morning at the end of the battle. We had just relieved a unit which had captured an enemy strongpoint known as Tower Hamlets. Just before dawn I went up to visit the three concrete pillboxes which constituted the strongpoint. The view ahead, as dawn and a rising mist revealed it, filled me with the greatest uplift I had experienced throughout the war. There far below us was the promised land. We had reached the summit of the ridge. Cultivated land, yes, actually cultivated land was shining in the sun, a patchwork of dark and light green fields. At intervals, farmhouses surrounded with trees, almost undamaged, lay peacefully quiet. Did this mean we had won through and were now clear of the mud in which we had been wallowing for weeks? I could see no signs of any enemy. Had they withdrawn? Was this the beginning of the end? Such were my hopes though I knew full well that they were little more than wishful thinking. But in any case, apart from any military significance, this peaceful scene was so beautiful that I just stood and drank it in and closed my eyes, trying to fix it in memory so that later I could recall the scene and enjoy it at will.

At the time Hudson was unable to think of anything apart from the immediate problems he faced but in later years he studied the personality and actions of Haig. He remarked:

It is difficult to see how Haig, as Commander-in-Chief living in the atmosphere he did, so divorced from the fighting troops, could fulfil the tremendous task that was laid upon him effectively. I did not believe then, and I do not believe now that the enormous casualties were justified. Throughout the war huge bombardments failed again and again yet we persisted in employing the same hopeless method of attack. Many other methods were possible, some were in fact used but only half-heartedly. Our sudden unheralded attack at Cambrai was not followed up; the German success on 21 March 1918 was said to be largely due to the fog and our lightly held front; an attack at night on a quiet sector would have produced similar conditions. Tunnelling under the enemy wire on a large scale would have got over the need for the destruction of the forward defences by a bombardment which made the ground impassable. Planned withdrawal, followed by a planned counter-attack, would have raised political difficulties and military risks, but how great were the possibilities. The politicians thought only in terms of strategy, of avoiding casualties by finding some distant way round the stalemate on the Western Front. Had either the French or ourselves been able to find a general of a calibre required, the stalemate could have been overcome tactically. The one hopeless tactic, the mass bombardment, which was repeatedly tried, was proved again and again to be fruitless.

Hudson also wrote:

Many years later, in 1930, my wife and I were travelling back from Singapore. At Colombo the Great War Prime Minister, David Lloyd George, his wife and daughter and a personal doctor, joined the ship. Lloyd George was recovering from an operation but was full of vigour, too full, his gentle wife seemed to think, for he would stamp around the decks, his short legs shooting out aggressively in spite of the weight which they seemed so inadequately designed to carry. He was writing his war memoirs and had reached the chapter in which the clash with Lord Haig was dealt with.

Enquiring one day about my war service, he asked if I had been at Paschendaele and what I, as a fighting soldier, thought of it. Few could resist his wonderful personal charm. I wanted to agree with him, and in many ways I did. No one in their senses could believe that a general, who really knew what the conditions at the front were, could have insisted on blundering on through that impossible morass. Some better way of achieving the object in view could surely have been found. I had long felt this, but an innate sense of loyalty made me hesitate to say so. L.G. was far too shrewd a judge of his fellow men to be deceived.

'The trouble with you soldiers,' he said, 'is always the same. Whatever the rights or wrongs of any question you will always back each other up. All the same,' he added, 'I have yet to meet anyone who actually fought at Paschendaele who did not believe the battle to have been a terrible mistake.'

With that, he dismissed the subject. Personally, I know nothing of Lord Haig. I had never seen him but I believe him to have been a man of high moral quality though I had been told that he was quite unable to get down to the level of the men. There was the story of how his staff had told him, before some inspection, that he must try to speak personally to a proportion of men on parade. Conscientiously trying to follow this advice, he said in a friendly tone to an obviously old soldier.

'Well, my man, where did you start the war?' To which the man, looking rather aggrieved, replied, 'I didn't start the war.'

After this the General passed on down the ranks without any attempt at conversation. And another story of how he visited some young officers doing a tactical course: he said he had little time to spare and could not go into the detail of the tactical scheme which they were studying, but would give them some general advice based on his own experience of war. He proceeded to enlarge on the theme that in war everything depended on being able to move faster than the enemy. As he left, he turned to the instructor and said: 'By the way, what is the theme of the scheme you are studying?' To which the instructor, looking rather embarrassed, replied: 'The withdrawal, Sir.'

After Paschendaele, Hudson was sent on a long course at the Senior Officers' School in England.

FIVE

· · · · · · · · ·

Italy

Hudson was just 25 and very young to be on a Senior Officers' Course. He had, almost miraculously, survived unscathed the Ypres salient, the Somme, Passchendaele and Messines. Men followed him. He was certainly not fearless. He understood the constant peril of death, but he seemed to be imbued with a determination to take some kind of positive action whatever the circumstances. At times he clearly was foolhardy, such as blowing into the chink in the German dugout. But these actions were more of an escape from the normal ghastly environment in which the front-line soldiers were living than an expression of mindless arrogance. He loved his country with all the fervour of nineteenth and early twentieth-century patriotism which his upbringing and experience had instilled in him. As he put it, later, in a poem:

England

England, a poem in a single word,
As to a lover whispering low the name
Of his beloved, again, again. A cord
That binds and, chafing, sets my heart aflame

As lovers wishing openly to claim
Their love by very mention of a name.
To them the name itself is beautiful,
The name that conjures up a perfect grace
And all the images that lovers dutiful
Will ponder on, the details of a face,
Those fascinating ways, those moods, nor space
Nor time can dim the beauty that they trace.

So England lives and ever will remain
For me and England's sons, our own fair land.
So England lives and ever will retain
Our constant love. The ever present band
Of sea that circles her, the cliffs, the sand,
The tiny fields so neatly chequer planned.

England a poem in a single word,
Her wealds, her lakes, her open plains, her hills,
Diversity, that sheath enfolds a sword
That gives a force to love, but piercing fills
Our hearts with shame to see the awful ills
Of slums and factories and smoke grimed hills.

Poets have sung of Spring, its vibrant life,
Of Winter's tracery that's etched each year
Against the sky, or sunlit sleepy mere,
Or Summer's woodland scene with startled deer
Standing alert filled with their age-long fear.

Artists have sketched, and later tried to paint
Those scenes that poets build in gifted lines
And yet to nature's truth there are but faint
Resemblances between what man designs
And all that love which in her own confines
England has stored, deep in her secret mines.

He accepted the logic of military discipline but, paradoxically, was ready to disregard orders when he thought he saw a fleeting opportunity for offensive action. He was far from a military automaton, able to appreciate beauty when it existed and to focus his mind on matters other than the obscenities around him. Like much of mankind, his personality was complex and often contradictory. At first he was overwhelmed by the heavy responsibilities he carried, but he came to accept these without too much internal anguish, although, as his poem 'Victory' makes clear, he was starkly aware of death.

Victory

They said 'We've won the battle
The enemy have fled,
Those that could flee
The rest are dead.'

A wire 'Congratulations'
Came through 'Your well fought fight.'
They said 'We'll celebrate,
Then sleep tonight.'

Oh hateful jubilations,
All that was done
Is worthless, now
My friend is dead.

His poem 'War' strikes a Shakespearean chord of beauty amid the squalor.

War

The modern poets say that war's all dirt,
They fear romance and say it's otherwise.

They need not seek to disillusion men
Who've fought, but only those who stayed at home,
Or going, never heard a bullet crack
The way for these is comradeship in death,
'We few, we happy few, we band of brothers.'
There find in one short line the truth of it
For fighting men. The cruelty, the blood,
The senselessness, the stricken families,
They know are there in stark intensity,
But in this cauldron of revoltant fear
A soldier, forced to dip, will find this pearl
Before he dies or sees his comrades die.

He had only been on the course for ten days when, having just received news of the award of a bar to his DSO, he received peremptory orders to return to his battalion to take over command of it as from 7 November 1917. The whole of his division had been ordered to Italy under command of General Plumer. At the time they had no idea why this was happening, but it later became apparent that they were there to support the Italians who had been defeated at Caporetto in the mountains north of Venice and were in full flight.

The battalion went to Italy in two trains, detraining at Mantua. They then marched to the River Piave hoping to get there before the enemy did. The march was made on a paved road and the soldiers' feet suffered badly, having been used to the mud of Belgium. As they marched on the right of the road the defeated Italian Army struggled down the left. No sort of order was maintained and no arms were carried.

The men were terribly emaciated and practically starving. At first our men began calling out friendly encouragement but the Italians were too dispirited to respond and for mile after mile we marched by each other in an embarrassed silence. Nearer the front we began to meet wagons packed with soldiery and drawn by horses that filled us with horror. The poor beasts could only just stagger; their rib bones were clearly visible, their eyes were glazed and when their merciless drivers flogged them on, our men angrily remonstrated and some ugly situations were narrowly averted. Later we passed groups of men gathered round fires and realised that a horse's misery ended when it fell exhausted, was dragged aside and was delivered to the pot. On one occasion we had fallen out for a normal short halt when a civilian open carriage of extreme decrepitude, drawn by well-fed and groomed horses, came trotting by. The occupants were four equally well-fed and groomed Italian officers in sky-blue uniforms and gold braid. The contrast between these Italian officers and their starving men was too much for some of our men; some booed, others cat-called. This exhibition of discourtesy to our allies, however much justified, could not be countenanced and by trotting close behind the equipage I was able by gestures to check our own men, but I could not fail to note the raised fists of the angry Italian soldiery as the carriage passed.

When they reached the River Piave there was no sign of the enemy. The battalion took over a battalion position from an Italian regiment. For a week or so the soldiers lived on Italian rations – breakfast was a cup of black bitter coffee and some hard biscuits, lunch was a mountain of spaghetti, in which was hidden a morsel of doubtful meat, and a mug of wine. Supper was the same as breakfast. The Italian officers, on the other hand, did themselves very well and Hudson had lunch with them, having difficulty after lunch in persuading them to show him round the trenches. Apparently no officer knew his way and eventually a senior NCO was found to guide him.

The defence scheme was explained:

On being heavily attacked the soldiers in the front line were to withdraw to the second line. The soldiers in the second line, on being heavily attacked were to withdraw to the third line. The document did not say who was to decide whether or not an attack was 'heavy'. Something of course had to be left to the imagination. An excellent sketch accompanied the scheme and on this was shown in varying colours the trenches that had been dug and those that as yet were only projected. I asked what happened when the third line was reached, upon which the Commanding Officer rose from the table, flung his cloak back over his shoulders with a magnificent gesture and said, 'In the third line we die for Italy.' At this the attendant headquarters' officers all cried 'Bravo'. I forbore to point out that the trench in which they were to die for Italy had not yet been dug.

Hudson became very fond of the Italians, but regarded their martial fervour, when it occurred, as something of a joke. He used to tell of how it was eventually decided that they would make an attack. The attacking group was together in a trench waiting for zero hour. The minutes and then seconds ticked by and when the moment came the officers drew their swords and leapt forward over the parapet. The soldiers, however, stayed where they were, applauding. 'Bravo, Bravissimo!' they shouted.

The battalion spent two and a half months in that area of Italy. It was a pleasant break. Total casualties were one officer, two other ranks killed and ten other ranks wounded. 'About what might be expected in one short tour in the trenches of France or Belgium in a quiet sector.'

In the middle of February 1918 the battalion was sent to take over from an Italian regiment on the Asiago plateau in the mountains of northern Italy near Granezza. In order not to make it obvious to the enemy that the British had taken over, they donned Italian helmets and lived for a short time on Italian rations. It was bitterly cold. The new trenches were cut in many places through solid rock. They ran along the fir-clad slopes overlooking a broad grassland plateau on the far side of which rose a high mountain barrier held by the enemy.

Routine life on the plateau was pleasant enough and except for occasional shellings there was little to remind them of war. There was no question of home leave but local leave was given about every three months. A leave camp was established at the southern extremity of Lake Garda, the northern end of which was held by the Austrians. A line of buoys across the lake marked the agreed boundary between the British and the Austrians. An Austrian patrol vessel patrolled on the far side but never fired on our sailing boats provided we remained on our side of the buoys.

Hudson went to the leave camp several times.

While lunching in the pleasant officers' club overlooking the lake, a party of staff officers came in. Their advent caused quite a stir, for among them was a slender, fresh complexioned and elegant young officer dressed in a style of uniform all his own. He had a curious air of shyness and visibly flushed when a hush followed his entrance. The Prince of Wales was in our midst.

For his only leave in Italy, apart from his three days on Lake Garda, Hudson went to Rome and Florence in the company of his American doctor. In Rome they stayed at a pretentious hotel. There then ensued a totally hilarious game of golf.

One morning I was somewhat flattered when the elder of two beautiful young American girls asked if by any chance I played golf. The Americans and their mother occupied an expensive suite in the hotel, and had never deigned to cast so much as a glance in our direction before. It seemed I was wanted to complete a foursome. The other man was to be the diplomatic representative of a South American state, a person, I was given to understand, of considerable standing, great wealth and ambassadorial rank. At first I thought I was wanted as an adjunct to a carefully staged matchmaking enterprise, but I was wrong. The girls, keen golfing enthusiasts, really wanted exercise on a golf course if only to keep their figures slim. It turned out their hearts were not set on the ambassador but on his car. Petrol rationing in Rome was very strict and even in diplomatic circles only the highest-ranking members could use a car for pleasure. The golf course was some way out, buses were too plebeian and taxis did not exist. In angling for the use of the ambassador's car they had asked him to play, never dreaming he would accept. To their mingled horror and amusement he had accepted and now they had to find a fourth. Would I mind?

That afternoon we drove out in great state; the car called at an imposing house to pick up the ambassador who had attended an official luncheon party there. He was wearing a morning coat and check trousers (pants to the Americans) but told us he intended to change into clothing more suitable for 'sport' at the golf club. He also said he hoped that he would not find the golf game too difficult, he had not tried before. No doubt, he added, he would be able to get himself fitted out with the necessary balls and sticks at the golf house. The girls, to whom he had so far addressed himself exclusively, being incapable of speech, I murmured that I had no clubs either and would have to hire. He pointed out that as he intended to take the game up seriously in future, he would buy all he would require now, and was gracious enough to say that he would be glad of my assistance in the matter.

At the clubhouse the Americans vanished into the ladies' cloakroom and I left the ambassador to change while I went over to the pro's hut. On my return the ambassador was arrayed in a canary-coloured pullover, a small white canvas cap perched precariously and centrally on the top of his head, white tennis shoes and check trousers. As I joined him on the verandah the sisters emerged, but only for a moment, for at the sight of him they were overcome with giggles and hastily retired again.

The ambassador and I went over to the pro's shop where the pro made hay while the sun so obviously shone. Our reappearance was heralded by a great assembly of diminutive caddies, to one of whom the pro handed over an outsize leather golf bag bulging with clubs. The only control I had been able to exercise was to defer the purchase of a left-handed club until further experience should prove its necessity. I had bought a few 'repaints', but for the ambassador a second caddy was entrusted with the duty of carrying a box of a dozen of the most expensive balls in the shop.

Our partners joined us at the first tee, still in a shaky state but sufficiently in command of themselves to be able to drive their balls firmly and surely down the centre of the fairway. We were all to drive, but only the longest ball of each partnership was to be subsequently played. It was the ambassador's turn and a formidable driver was handed him. He addressed the ball in a fair but awkward imitation of the stances adopted by our partners. Refusing to take any preliminary practice shot he asked which of a row of fore caddies he should aim at? Then with a prodigious swing he made a complete air shot. The girls were behind him and one who had already nearly swallowed her handkerchief in her efforts to suppress her laughter was unable to speak, but the other and myself hastily agreed that a miss did not count.

Another air shot followed, and, as we held our breath, at the third shot he struck the ground about a foot behind the ball with such force that we feared he must have broken his wrist. Whether he thought the anguished cries from the girls were in sympathy with him or not, I do not know, but his blood was up and only when pure exhaustion intervened did he give up and decide that he would select his own club from the formidable bag. He chose a putter. Once more he stood menacingly and more directly over the stationary ball. At the second or third shot and without once touching the ground he hit the ball a very creditable whack straight down the course. He turned to his partner with a pleased smile.

'It would have been better,' he said, 'if the ball had gone into the air. They don't seem to have cut the grass in front of the tee.'

From now on he insisted on using his putter, explaining that he would learn the use of the other ten or dozen clubs in his bag, later. Reluctantly he agreed to the ball being teed up whenever it was his turn, for by this means we hoped to reduce the carnage which his frequent onslaughts on the fairway were making.

It was already getting dark when we came to a very short hole. The tee shot was over a deep, narrow gully spanned farther down by an old Roman viaduct. On the far side lay the green, well guarded by bunkers except immediately opposite the tee. My partner's ball landed on the slope and rolled ignominiously back into the gully. My ball and the ambassador's partner's ball landed in the bunker well beyond the green. The ambassador hit his ball hard and clean. It ricocheted off the slope into the air at a remarkably steep angle and landing just short of the hole rolled slowly forward, coming to rest on the very lip of the tin. This feat was greeted with loud applause, which the ambassador accepted with a delighted smile and the removal of his diminutive cap.

As I followed the party down into the gully I remembered I had left my tee peg behind. Returning to retrieve it I was just in time to see a caddie, who must have been taking cover in a bunker, dart across the green, tip the ambassador's ball into the hole and nip back out of sight. My partner had some trouble driving her ball out of the rough, during which time I was able to tell both girls what I had seen. As we breasted the steep rise the disappearance of the ambassador's ball was met with astonishment and dismay which turned into loud cries of delight when a caddy, running forward, lifted a ball from the hole itself, and held it triumphantly aloft.

The ambassador was somewhat overcome by the excitement caused by the crowd of caddies, assistant caddies and miscellaneous onlookers who seemed to spring up from all sides. He asked if holing out in one hit was very unusual. A spokesman caddy, apparently reputed to speak English, was pushed forward from the crowd. By the use of a few English words, such as 'good-morning', 'goodnight', accompanied by a wealth of gesture, he soon made it plain that the occasion demanded special acknowledgement in the form of a gratuity to all who had witnessed this remarkable feat, and in particular himself. Though agreeing in principle with the main contention, each of the others proceeded to refute any special claim to consideration put forward by anyone other than themselves and, as is the way with small boys the world over, the meeting soon broke up into a seething mass of individual wrestling matches. It was a memorable day, ending with liberal potions of champagne in the bar.

In sharp contrast to the golf match the action was now approaching where Hudson was to win his Victoria Cross (VC) and to receive his first wound. His battalion was to hold a sector of the front line on the San Sisto ridge. An attack was to be mounted through their position, which they were to follow up. The French were on their right. On the near side of the ridge the ground was steep but on the enemy side the ground sloped more gently through fir trees to the front line which ran just inside the edge of the woods. Two companies held the front trench, a third was on the top of the ridge and the fourth was in reserve behind the ridge. Battalion headquarters was in a quarry behind the ridge just below the top. In the year 1998 when the author visited it, the whole area was exactly as it was in 1918. Even the trenches were totally undisturbed.

On 14 June information came through that two Czechs, one a doctor, had deserted to the French and had categorically affirmed that the enemy would attack on the morning of 15 June and that the main axis of attack would be precisely where the 11th Sherwood Foresters were situated. There was no doubt about the information, which had been corroborated by other means. There was to be a four-hour bombardment, including gas, followed by a dawn attack.

The bombardment started punctually at 3 a.m. The enemy was using heavy calibre guns and there was the sweet smell of gas. A heavy Italian mortar battery had been established in a tunnelled position close to the battalion headquarters. Hudson went to see them in order to ask for help. As he entered, the battery was ordered to come to attention. Unfortunately most of them were trouserless as they were in the act of donning rubber drawers as a protection against gas, as the battery commander put it: 'The future of Italy had to be borne in mind.' In the event, for various reasons, the mortar battery was not of much help.

Hudson's intelligence officer was able to climb a tree and he saw dense columns of enemy infantry led by an officer on a white horse advancing across the plateau towards the ridge. A number of men were pushing bicycles. Hudson sent his second-in-command to bring up the reserve company. He evacuated his headquarters, which was in a very vulnerable position. Cooks, batmen, signallers and sanitary men were spread out in a rough line pending the arrival of the reserve company. Hudson sent his Italian liaison officer to visit the French on the right to find out what was happening there. He returned, very upset, to say that the French had withdrawn and Hudson's battalion's flank was completely exposed. Fire began to be directed on the battalion headquarters from the ridge above. It was clear that, in some areas at least, the enemy had broken through the front line. Gathering what men he could find – mostly the battalion headquarters' staff – Hudson advanced up the ridge in order to attack the enemy who had broken through. He went on alone along the remains of the front line trench. He came on a wounded Austrian soldier lying full length on the fire step.

He was a middle-aged man and deathly pale. On seeing me apparently threatening him with my rifle he mumbled something and attempted to raise his hand in token of surrender, but he was too weak and his arms fell pathetically back. To reassure him I lowered my rifle and smiled but placed my finger on my lips to indicate silence. Relieved, he gave me a wan smile, and we looked into each other's eyes. I do not think that the utter futility of war had ever been more strongly borne in upon me as I gazed at this wounded enemy soldier. His wounds had been bound up, and as I bent over him he shook his head, as much as to say there is nothing to be done and his eyes closed.

The echo of the Walt Whitman poem 'Reconciliation' (see page 22) is remarkable.

Hudson sent for his reserve company to join him in order to make a counter-attack at a crucial moment. He was joined by a sergeant who, without waiting for orders, jumped to his feet and rushed forward towards the Austrian line. He was shot and collapsed on the ground. Hudson then advanced himself and

I found myself standing over our own front line looking down on some twenty or thirty Austrians in the trench below. I shouted in English 'Hands up!' and those who had their backs towards me turned, others sitting on the fire step rose and some, who were eating, continued to sit stolidly where they were; all, however, with one exception, raised their hands above their head. . . . One or two of the men began lowering their hands slowly and I threatened them again, trying to appear master of the situation and wondering how on earth I was going to extricate myself. . . .
In an effort to create the impression that I was supported, I shouted back over my shoulder, telling my imaginary troops to stay where they were. Then I beckoned an officer out of the trench towards me. He was a feeble, untidy looking creature wearing spectacles and he came obediently out of the trench. As he approached I stepped slowly back as far as I dared, but I could not afford to lose sight of the men in the trench. This was a mistake, for in a flash a truculent-looking NCO bobbed down out of sight. . . . A tremendous explosion blew me into the air. How I could have missed noticing a stick bomb drop on my feet I do not know. . . . I tried to get up but could not.

Hudson rolled and dropped into the trench. Two bombs exploded just above him. He fainted. At that moment a platoon from one of the forward companies arrived and, having recovered his senses, Hudson was taken back on a stretcher to his battalion headquarters. He fainted again before he reached the headquarters, but came to and insisted on directing the reserve company and another company which had been sent forward to help in a counter-attack.

Hudson's adjutant was very upset at his condition because the doctor had told him that he was unlikely to live and would in any case lose a leg.

'Partly to comfort him, and partly to show that I was not done yet,' wrote Hudson, 'I challenged him to a game of chess while we awaited the arrival of the company but it was not long before I had to abandon the game.'

The counterattack came off and was highly successful. The battalion ended the day with its position intact, having captured 4 officers, 152 other ranks, 5 flame-throwers, a trench mortar and 8 machine guns. The British losses during the day were only 1 officer killed and 3 wounded, 7 other ranks killed and 41 wounded with 3 missing.

Hudson was evacuated, first to a casualty clearing station, then to a hospital in Genoa, then by ambulance train to Marseilles and finally by boat to London and a small hospital in Mount Street, London. At Genoa Hospital he was awoken by a surgeon who told him that he would probably die if he did not agree to the amputation of a leg. Bloody minded as ever, Hudson refused the offer and went to sleep again. (He did not lose his leg.) He was appalled at the change from real devoted care at the front gradually deteriorating into mindless bureaucracy further back from the front. However, his final destination in the small private hospital was very different. He was nursed by a charming Voluntary Aid Detachment (VAD), who later became his adored and adoring wife.

1. Charles Hudson (sitting) with his mother, brother Tommy and sister Dolly.

2. Charles (left) with siblings Tommy and Dolly.

3. Charles's father, Herbert Hudson.

4. Brabyn's Hall, near Stockport in Cheshire.

5. The house in Newent in the Forest of Dean where Charles lived until he was 7 years old.

6. Charles's mother in the family carriage at Newent in the Forest of Dean.

7. Soldiers cut a communications trench in the remains of Delville Wood on the Somme. *(IWM Q4417)*

8. On the Somme, men of 7th Division are silhouetted against the chalk lines marking the trenches covering Mametz. *(IWM Q87)*

9. Charles as a young soldier in Sherwood Foresters uniform.

10. British troops prepare to go over the top. (IWM Q5098)

11. Trench life in the First World War. (IWM Q4654)

12. Asiago plateau in the mountains of northern Italy: looking from Cesuna, in the British lines, towards the village of Rotzo behind the Austrian lines. *(John Chester)*

13. British trenches in the Montello sector overlooking the River Piave, Italy. *(IWM Q26115)*

14. Gladys, wife of Charles Hudson.

15. Charles and
Gladys Hudson.

16. Charles and
Gladys on a skiing
holiday with (far left)
Charles's sister-in-
law Bertha.

17. Charles in the uniform of King's Own Scottish Borderers.

18. Charles as Brigadier.

19. Charles with Lady Mountbatten receiving the St John Award.

A few weeks later a staff officer of my division, known as the White Rabbit, called to see me, out of visiting hours. He said his business was of the most urgent nature, and I was much amused for the White Rabbit always managed to invest his doings in a shroud of mystery and importance. It was however very good of him to have hunted me out, and I asked that he might be allowed up. After preliminary greetings he gave me to understand that his mission was a very secret one involving personages of the highest rank. Glancing round the ward he whispered that I must give him my word that I would not breathe a word of what he was about to tell me until his secret had become public. In that case, I said, would it not be better to wait until that moment? His face fell and he was so obviously disappointed that I relented and gave him the assurance he required. He then told me that my name had been submitted for the Victoria Cross. He had been to the War Office and the recommendation would be placed before the King on the following morning, but until His Majesty's approval had been given, the matter had to be regarded as strictly confidential.

I was completely flabbergasted. He said recommendations had to be supported by two eye-witnesses, and explained how he had gone personally to the prisoners' cages in Italy and had ferreted out Austrian prisoners to support the recommendation sent in. The British sergeant had already been awarded a DCM, and the delay in my case had been due to the time taken in finding the witnesses. Next day I received official notification of the award, and with it the information that the Italian High Command had given me the Italian Croce Di Valori in silver, which, I was informed, was the highest award open to a foreigner. It seemed to me that the whole thing was being rather overdone, but at least I could assume that the honour was paid as much to the battalion as it was to me personally.

The only officer killed in that action was Edward Brittain, the famous author Vera Brittain's adored brother. Just before the battle Hudson had been told by the Provost Marshall that a letter from an officer in the battalion to another in the same company had been censored at the base and that from the context of the letter it was unmistakably clear that the two were involved in homosexual activity with men in their company. One of them was Edward Brittain. This was an extremely serious crime with a maximum penalty of ten years' penal servitude. Hudson was told to avoid letting the officers become aware of what was known since further enquiries were being pursued, but to keep an eye on them. Hudson did not approve, as he saw it, of spying on his own officers: 'He had been loyal to me and it seemed disloyal to him to play cat and mouse with him.'

In fact, he did give Edward Brittain a strong hint of the situation by saying to him: 'I did not realise that letters written out here were censored at the base.' Brittain made no comment but went very white.

Brittain was found shot in the head and Hudson wondered if he had in fact killed himself or deliberately exposed himself in order to get killed. He was highly intelligent, a man with a very loving family who would have been shattered if he had been court-martialled for homosexuality with men under his command. The possibility of suicide was clearly there.

Later, when Hudson was in hospital, Vera Brittain visited him and asked him exactly what had happened. Hudson tried to console her by telling her that her brother had suffered no pain being shot through the head, but she became extremely angry, perhaps sensing Hudson's embarrassment. She did not believe him and was certain that he was holding something back. She pursued him for days, even writing a poem hinting that Brittain had deserved the VC no less than had Hudson, and that Hudson was covering something up. The last verse read as follows:

> 'Tis not your valour's meed alone you bear
> Who stands the hero of a nation's pride;

For on that humble cross you live to wear
Your friends were crucified.

In her book *Testament of Youth* Vera Brittain characterised Hudson as 'ambitious and intrepid, the son of a Regular Army officer who could not afford to equip him for a peacetime commission [author's note – this is of course quite wrong], the young man had found in the War the fulfilment of his baffled longing for military distinction.'

She went on to talk of his 'hard young face' and, with his VC, of his 'sitting on the pinnacle of his martial ambitions – a stiff young disciplinarian, impregnated with all the military virtues but limited in imagination and benevolence.' At no stage at that time did Hudson even hint at the real reason for his embarrassment and hesitation. In fact, as Hudson later found out, it was very likely that Brittain had in fact died when going forward up the hill to find out what was happening to a platoon of his which was out on an outpost in no man's land. The truth will never be known. Vera Brittain, however, persisted in her view that Hudson was denying her brother recognition for some act of gallantry.

Much later, after reading *Testament of Youth*, Hudson thought that Vera might well want to know what had really happened. He wrote to her suggesting a meeting, which she accepted. 'It is quite possible that had my brother survived the War he might have told me whatever facts you have to relate,' she said

They met on 9 July 1933 in her house in Chelsea and Hudson told her the truth. It was a great shock to her, but she resolutely refused to entertain the idea that Edward had committed suicide and held to the belief that he had died when carrying out some heroic act. She may well have been right. However, she accepted his homosexual leanings. This was confirmed later in 1937 when her mother told her that she had found a diary of Edward's while he was at Uppingham which clearly confirmed his sexual proclivities. It is a sad story.

SIX

• • • • • •

The Final Advance
and Russia

When in hospital Hudson was told that his command would automatically lapse three months after he was wounded. He was keen to get back to his battalion before the three months were up and this entailed passing a Medical Board. Unfortunately all efforts to graft skin onto a wound in his foot had failed. He could walk but with some discomfort. He thought it unlikely that the Medical Board would pass him fit for active service but nevertheless he tried. To his surprise he passed, later discovering that the Chairman of the Board had persuaded his colleague to pass him on the argument that having got a VC, two DSOs and an MC, he was clearly determined to get himself killed and they may as well let him get on with it.

When he reached Calais, to his astonishment he was told that he had been appointed to command the second battalion of his regiment, which was serving in France, and that he was to report direct to the battalion which was one of the only two regular battalions in the regiment. This was a great shock, not only because he was very young – just 26 – but because regular battalions were normally commanded by officers with far more than his very limited military experience of only three and a half years.

On his arrival on 20 September 1918 he found that the battalion had just withdrawn from one of their heaviest actions in the war in which they had lost in killed, wounded and missing nearly 400 officers and men. Furthermore, the commanding officer, a very gallant soldier, had just been ordered to report to the Corps School as commandant. The implication that he had failed in some way was unavoidable and Hudson's arrival was the final straw in his discomfiture. To add to Hudson's difficulties, the divisional general made it clear that he had great doubts as to his suitability for command and that he had asked for another officer who, unfortunately, was not available. Hudson's interviews with his new brigade and divisional commanders were, as he put it in his journal, 'very chilling experiences'.

The commanding officer who had been superseded was, nevertheless, extremely helpful. A fortnight after Hudson's arrival the battalion was called on to go into action. He knew none of the remaining officers and during that fortnight many new officers and men had arrived. It must have been a difficult time for all concerned. They set out for the front on 4 October on a long march which crossed the Hindenburg Line. Hudson was astonished that the Germans had not defended these formidable obstacles and concluded that German morale must be at a very low ebb. He determined to push through any gap he found, secure in the knowledge that the enemy would be most unlikely to be able to mount a counter-attack.

The last month or so of the war was far from a quiet experience for the 2nd Sherwood Foresters. The battalion mounted a series of attacks and a number of officers and men were killed. Hudson was hit and knocked over by a fragment of shell which did not, however, penetrate his Sam Browne belt. Later, he was setting his map with a compass on the edge of a shell hole when a shell hit the lip and blew the map and compass high into the air without doing him any damage. He certainly had a charmed life.

At one stage he was with the leading company as usual when he saw through his field glass 1,000yd away two six-gun German batteries behind hedges. To his astonishment a young, immaculately dressed subaltern in highly-polished field boots appeared beside him. He said that he was from the Scots Greys, he had left his troop a short way behind and had come forward to get in touch with the leading infantry. Hudson told him that he had a chance that few cavalrymen had had in the history of war. Hudson's company could hold the attention of the German batteries while he took his troop round the flank and attacked the batteries from behind. The subaltern said that he had been told not to get involved in any fighting but to find out what was happening and report when a breakthrough had occurred. Hudson was reluctant to persuade him to disobey orders but, borrowing his orderly's horse, he rode back with him to his troop in order to lead them forward round the guns. On the way they saw the German guns limber up and disappear. He later discovered that, had the operation taken place as he had planned it, it would have been a disaster, as a concealed sunken road lay on the route which they would not have seen until they were right on it.

In the event, the battalion took its objective and had captured 5 German officers and 450 men, 6 field guns, 12 machine guns and a lot of other booty, but they had lost 9 officers and over 150 men. They were well ahead of the troops on their flanks.

Hudson spent the night in a German dugout, the head-quarters of a machine gun battalion. They had captured the commanding officer, who appeared in a sparkling uniform wearing white gloves. He was a thoroughly objectionable Prussian officer who blamed the scum of socialists at home for the disasters they were facing. Hudson's second visitor that night was:

about as different a personality as human nature was capable of producing on a field of battle. He introduced himself by shouting cheerily down the steps in a broad American accent. All he wanted, he explained, was a light and cover from the rain so as to read his map. He had lost his way, and he had left his battalion 'some ways back'. I asked him where he was making for and he pulled out three or four pages of closely typewritten orders. He said he had only read as far as a paragraph which told him to march his battalion to a certain map reference. He had not got there yet, but when he had he would read the rest of the order.

Hudson then went to sleep, fortunately wearing his gas mask. When he woke up he found that the second-in-command, the signals officer and a number of signallers, including the signaller sergeant, were practically blind from the effects of mustard gas. He had already lost his adjutant, killed in action, and at his headquarters he only had one very young intelligence officer. There were only two company commanders unwounded.

The advance continued. At one stage they were held up by heavy fire from a brickworks near the village of Vaux Andigny. Having succeeded in driving the Germans out, Hudson established his headquarters in the house owned by the manager of the brickworks. He implored Hudson to send his family, consisting of an elderly granny, his wife, a nurse and a little girl of 12, back to friends in the town of Bohain in Army transport. Hudson did so. Eleven years later there occurred an almost miraculous coincidence. While at the Staff College Hudson went on a battlefield tour with three other students, including the future General Brian Robertson. He suddenly recognised the brickworks and was persuaded to call in on the manager's house. The door was opened by a man in a dinner jacket who fell on his neck with pleasure and excitement. The little girl of 12 was now in her 20s and about to get married that very day. Her father had written to Hudson via the War

Office, but had got the name wrong and Hudson never received the letter. The manager was just about to leave for the wedding, having stayed behind the rest of his party to make some final arrangements. Clearly Hudson and his friends would have to attend.

As they arrived, the bride was anxiously standing at the door waiting for her father. The church was very crowded but, to their embarrassment, they were ushered to the front, clearly very incorrectly dressed in the circumstances. The manager and his friends did not believe that Hudson had not received his letter.

The next major battle undertaken by the battalion was on 23 October. The battalion had been reduced to an officer strength of eight. Hudson was sent four more officers, two of whom announced they were suffering from shellshock and were quickly sent home. The advance was slow, but eventually they succeeded in crossing the Oise Canal. They held the line along the river while other troops continued the advance.

In the village of Ors they found a British soldier who had been concealed in the attic of a cottage since 1914. The cottage had been searched many times, but he had avoided detection by lying at full length between the floor of one room and the ceiling of the one below. His saviour, the lady owner of the cottage, was in a terrible plight as was the British soldier, both emaciated beyond belief. Hudson never found out whether they survived.

Talk of the end of the war had been discouraged since, if they expected the war to end any minute, it would be very difficult to induce soldiers to take necessary or unnecessary risks. The end came as a complete surprise, the message reading: 'All hostilities will cease as from 11.00 tomorrow, 11 November. ACK.' (In Army terminology the last word demanded an acknowledgement).

No doubt like many others, Hudson found it impossible to rejoice.

I sat with my head in my hands while the tears welled up in my eyes and ran down my cheeks. So this is how war ends, I thought. Hundreds of my friends and comrades have suffered and died and I just write the letters – ACK.

The battalion had reached the town of Bohain. Many British soldiers, however, were not so restrained and it was not long before the whole town was in a state of hilarious delirium. The next morning, early, the German plenipotentiaries passed through the town in a decrepit Ford of the old high-seated type. In the back seat sat two resplendent German officers with their swords between their knees. Between them, looking rather sheepish and very scruffy in contrast, sat a British officer who had evidently come straight out of the line. The impression was the Germans were the victors and the British the vanquished.

At five minutes to eleven o'clock the Americans fired off all their guns, both artillery and machine guns. The British remained silent. The French were extremely angry at the damage to their countryside the gunfire must have made.

The battalion started a march to Cologne on 14 November. Having crossed the border, in one village a deputation headed by the mayor asked for an interview. The mayor, a very old man, had clearly been pushed into making a request which he expected to be refused. He explained that the following day was the anniversary of a battle fought in the war of 1870 in which a number of villagers had been killed. To mark the anniversary, ever since the battle the survivors put on their 1870 uniforms and marched at the head of a procession to the churchyard where a service was held at the war memorial. They wanted permission to conduct the ceremony as usual.

Hudson told them there would be no objection. The mayor then went on to ask if Hudson would give orders that there should be no interference or demonstration against the march by the British soldiers. Hudson replied he would give no such order since it would be quite unnecessary, for British soldiers would never dream of misbehaving themselves on such an occasion. The Germans remained doubtful. However, next morning the British soldiers stood watching the procession in complete silence. They were obviously touched. Behind the tattered flag came three old soldiers dressed in their 1870 uniforms. They held themselves proudly and behind them marched all the men of the village, wearing their mourning clothes. The women had assembled at the memorial and, throughout the march, the church bell tolled. In the event, as the procession passed, the British soldiers reverently removed their caps.

Shortly after the battalion arrived at its final billets on the outskirts of Cologne, Hudson had a severe attack of flu and was sent to hospital in England. On recovery he was given three months' leave and told that, since a number of officers senior to him had rejoined his battalion, he would revert to the rank of captain and would be lucky if he became second-in-command of a company. This was not a very attractive proposition and he went to the War Office to ask if he could be sent to Russia.

> I knew that there were several British Forces spread around the borders of Bolshevik Russia and I was curious to know what was going on, both in the military and the political sense. I had no idea what the political theories of the Bolsheviks were, but at any rate they certainly seemed worthy of investigation.

Hudson was told that there was no question of him going since, far from sending officers out to Russia, there was at that time a tendency to withdraw them. Hudson heard that ships for Russia normally sailed from Harwich, although he was told that the last convoy for Russia had already sailed. Nevertheless he went to Harwich and managed to persuade an American naval captain whose ship was due to sail to Murmansk in the north of Russia, to take him with him. He heard that Arctic clothing had been issued from the Tower of London. He went there and got himself fitted out with a mass of suitable kit without any questions being asked.

This intervention in Russia in 1918–20 was an extraordinary affair. Servicemen from sixteen countries including Britain, the United States, Japan and France entered Russia from the north, south, east and west initially in order to support those Russians (known as the Whites), who wished to continue the war against Germany, in their struggle against the revolutionary Reds who wanted to make a separate peace and to establish a Communist (Bolshevik) state. After the German surrender (when Hudson arrived) the intervention became a simple matter of support for the Whites against the Reds. It was a total failure on all fronts. The main British effort was in the north of Russia at Murmansk and Archangel. (Miles Hudson, *Intervention in Russia 1918–1920, A Cautionary Tale*)

The ship duly sailed for Murmansk, the American naval officers being very friendly to the only two non-Americans on board: a Canadian major and Hudson.

> It was exciting easing our way down the Kola River through the ice floes to Murmansk, then only a quay and a number of tin shanties. On arrival I went ashore to call on Command HQ in search of a job. I was passed on to the Chief Intelligence Officer, one Colonel Thornhill, who had been assistant military attaché in tsarist days and was a fluent Russian speaker. He told me he was looking for a British officer to lead a reconnaissance party of Russian partisans to gain contact with the White Finns on the Russo-Finnish border, a cross-country trek of about 100 miles. He refused my immediate acceptance of this mission, telling me I should sleep on it first. He then explained that, though he could more or less guarantee the loyalty of the interpreter he would provide, since he would certainly be shot if not tortured as well if he was caught by the Reds of either country, it was never possible to guarantee the loyalty of the partisans, who would change sides to suit themselves without a qualm.

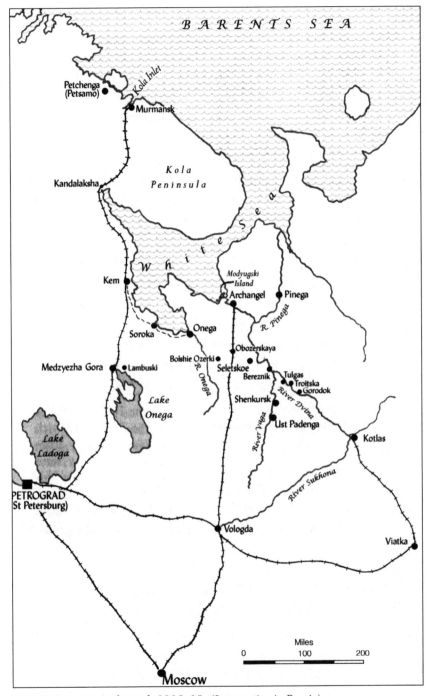

Russian Front at Archangel, 1918–19. *(Intervention in Russia)*

A rendezvous with the Finn Whites had been arranged but, there again, no one could tell for certain who in fact would turn up on the day appointed and if I were to fall into the hands of the Reds there was little if anything he could do about it if they chose to treat me as a spy. I was to return on the following day and if I still wanted to go, he would introduce me to the leader of the partisans and my interpreter.

On leaving Thornhill I went to see the harbour master to beg the use of a boat, for I had been invited to dinner at HQ ashore and my American captain had intimated he was very hard-pressed for boats.

The harbour master, a naval captain, was in a conference and I was shown into his private office to await his return. I had my back to the door when he burst in and began cursing me with a non-stop flow of lurid language. Who the hell was I? What was I doing in his private office? For all he knew I was a spy hoping to get a look at his secret papers. I seemed to be dealing with a madman and indeed, from what I heard afterwards, I very nearly was, for the Arctic winter had sent many men off their normal balance. I tried to mollify him, but was put under arrest and only after I had insisted on a phone call to Colonel Thornhill did I escape incarceration. My only consolation was that in the end I got my boat.

I told Thornhill the following day that I was still prepared to take a chance on the Finnish venture and transferring myself ashore I spent some days practising skiing whilst plans were discussed; but in the end, and not altogether to my regret, the whole expedition broke down because the partisans cried off.

It was Thornhill who told me that two teams of sleigh dogs, belonging to Shackleton of Antarctic fame, were being sent by the land route to Archangel and that if I cared to go with them he could arrange it. He told me, too, that I would have a much better chance of getting congenial employment on the Archangel front than at Murmansk. Gratefully I accepted the offer.

The two sleighs, with Russian drivers, were to start before light but, as was typical of Russian methods, it was some hours after dawn before we got off and then only on the strength of a liberal tip to the head driver.

It was a fine sunny day and the huskies ran with spirit, tugging at the traces, while the driver jumped on the skids at any slight decline in the normally level track. We had run a few miles, and the leading sleigh was already out of sight, when a small sleigh pulled by a reindeer and driven by an old Russian peasant, joined the track from the forest, about 50yd ahead of us. This encounter was too much both for the reindeer, a mangy old beast, and our huskies. The reindeer fled and before our driver could control them our dogs were in full cry. The small sleigh, loaded down with wood, hit a mound of snow on the side of the track, the traces broke, and the reindeer, freed, set off at full gallop across the country. My driver's shouts, as he clung desperately to the reins of my sleigh, only encouraged the excited team the more, and soon he was dragged off his feet and fell flat on his face in the snow. There was nothing I could do, enclosed as I was in a sack of straw, except hold on as best I could. Before long the sleigh turned over, the traces parted, and I was precipitated into the snow, sack and all, with a severe thump on the head from the overturned sleigh.

As the team disappeared among the trees I extricated myself from the sack, ruefully rubbed the back of my head and finally sat down on the upturned sleigh. I heard loud lamentations behind me and, turning, saw the Russian peasant stumbling through the snow, stopping at frequent intervals to cross himself. I offered him a cigarette, but he only moaned the louder. Some rouble notes did much to restore his equanimity and the last I saw of him he was plodding off in pursuit of his precious reindeer.

In the event, Hudson managed to get on the first ice-cutter to attempt the journey to Archangel through the frozen White Sea. After four days the vessel arrived at Archangel: 'Suddenly we rounded a bend in the river and saw the five green, white and gold cupolas of Archangel Cathedral. It was an enchanting sight.' Shortly after arrival Hudson was taken to see the formidable General Ironside, who commanded the British troops in North Russia.

Ironside was a big man who made use of his imposing presence in a big way. I was not too sure of my ground and the General's opening remark did little to reassure me.

'I gather,' he said, 'that you have come out here to bounce me into giving you a job, because you don't want to go back to your regiment.'

I told him I had not thought of it only in that way, but nevertheless I hoped I might be of some use to him although the War Office had told me no more British officers were wanted in North Russia. This set him off.

'They told you that!' he shouted, 'when in every cable I send them I ask for officers. But I want good ones and how am I to know that you are any good?'

I replied politely that I imagined he was fully capable of judging that for himself, and he grunted.

Eventually Hudson was appointed as Brigade Major to Brigadier General Turner, who had himself only recently come out to Russia. He commanded a force of all arms and various nationalities holding the railway line about 90 miles south of Archangel. Two other columns of Russian troops under British officers were also under General Turner, one on the Onega River, 60 miles to the west, and the other holding a place called Seletskoe, 30 miles to the east. Before he left, Hudson asked General Ironside to authorise his appointment with the War Office in London and to tell it that he was not a deserter.

Turner also had under his command a strong Polish machine gun company, two companies of Americans, some Russian engineers, a troop of Cossack cavalry and an armoured train manned by Russian sailors.

The headquarters was in the large village of Obozerskaya, with an outpost further south at the village of Bolshie Ozerki. In March the French officer in charge, Commandant Lucas, had heard of the approach towards Bolshie Ozerki of a Bolshevik column. According to his British staff, he sat down to write 'An Appreciation of the Situation', aided by liberal potions of brandy. As his morale alternately rose and fell as a result of the rumours of the strength of the enemy and the effects of the brandy, he destroyed and rewrote his conclusion. In between times he could be heard striding up and down his office compartment muttering, 'What would Foch do?' By nightfall he had decided not only that Foch would withdraw from the village, but that he would withdraw his headquarters' train from Obozerskaya to a siding 10 miles north. Orders were given that the train was to be prepared to move at short notice. The British staff were mortified by this order and 'the brigade major, staff captain and signals officer crept down to the engine at night and while one held the attention of the engine driver the others poured boiling water on the rails further down the line'. This, they had been told, would have the effect of spinning the icebound wheels of the engine when it reached the doctored track. The Bolshevik column, if it existed, never turned up and the next day General Ironside replaced Commandant Lucas with Brigadier General Turner.

Our force included a few aged aeroplanes and in one of these I went over to visit our column on the Onega River. It was the first time I had ever flown. The Bristol Fighter was piloted by a young British officer and as the only other seat was that of the rear-gunner, I had perforce to undertake his duty. Bolshevik planes were very rarely seen on our front, but there was always the off-chance that we might encounter one. The rear-gunner's machine gun was attached to a rail which ran round the back of my small compartment. When we got into the air I picked up the gun, to make sure I could operate it, and seeing we were about to fly over a lake in the forest, I thought I would test myself and the gun by firing a burst at the lake surface. To do this I had to stand up and lean well out, in order to depress the muzzle of the gun sufficiently to aim at the lake. As soon as I fired, the aeroplane swept abruptly up at a high angle into the air and almost at the same time I had the impression that the ground was rushing up towards me. I realised when we landed that the pilot had performed some sort of acrobatic feat, and I accused him of trying to be funny and frighten me out of my wits, which indeed he had.

He explained that he had only carried out the correct action as taught at the time. When the rear-gunner fired, the pilot had to assume that an enemy aircraft was on his tail; he therefore automatically looped the loop with the object of placing his own machine on the tail of the attacker and shooting him down with his forward gun. I had, in fact, been far too frightened to realise we had looped the loop.

On the evening of 20 July, Hudson was working in his office just before dinner when his chief clerk, a Russian, crept in furtively, keeping below the level of the windows. The blind having been drawn at the chief clerk's request, he said that a note had been handed to him by a Russian private soldier, obviously having mistaken him for a Russian sergeant major in one of the reserve battalions to whom it had been addressed. The note made it clear that the enemy would attack on the railway at dawn on 23 July. The two White Russian battalions in the line would offer no resistance and would arrest their officers just before the attack, shooting any who resisted. The writer, who signed with a code name, said that he anticipated no difficulty in overrunning the remainder of the brigade who would be taken entirely by surprise, and for this reason only the forward battalions had been informed of the plan. The note also said that a special column which was to attack Force Headquarters was already in position in the forest and that the recipient of the note had to arrange to cut a gap in the wire, at the place arranged, during the night preceding the attack. In a final paragraph the writer said that arrangements had been made for communications to be cut in good time.

The only absolutely reliable troops were about twenty British at headquarters, the Polish company of machine-gunners and, possibly, the crew of the armoured train who were Russian sailors and, as such, on bad terms with the Russian soldiers.

It was clearly vital to relieve the two forward battalions as soon as possible. Having finished the dinner as normal, in order not to excite the suspicion of the Russians who were serving them, a plot was hatched. The plan was that two reserve battalions would be paraded and told that cholera had broken out in the two forward battalions and that relief would be carried out by train, company by company, immediately after the parade. As each forward battalion approached the station, which would be surrounded by the Polish machine-gunners, the men would be told that the armoured train had broken down, blocking the line, and they were to get out of the train, leaving their equipment behind them. They would then be disarmed and marched to prisoner of war cages under Polish escort. If any attempt to resist was made, the armoured train and the Poles would be used to overpower them. The senior White Russian colonel would be in charge.

The whole affair went exactly according to plan. Eight times the manoeuvre was put into operation and every time it worked smoothly. However, it remained important to find the names of the leaders of the conspiracy. As each company was disarmed, the Russian colonel asked for the names of these men. When no one volunteered any information he told them he would pick on any man in the ranks, count ten men down from him and that man would be shot. When the first batch of men was singled out, a Polish party marched them away into the forest. This was followed by a burst of fire. Hudson, who was observing, although he knew that the men were not being shot, was staggered by the phlegmatic way in which the majority of the men, even those who knew they were about to be shot, faced their apparent fate. At intervals, for hour after hour, this process went on. It was getting on for ten o'clock that night when the last company was marched away and still no information was forthcoming. Hudson wrote in his journal:

> As the last company passed us, a young boy, a bugler, broke away and approached the colonel and myself and, having been promised a release from the Army and a return to his village, told us who the ringleaders were.

When the Bolsheviks attacked on the morning of 23 July they were faced by the reserve battalions which had been moved to the Front and which repulsed the attack. As for the potential mutineers, after heavy interrogation, including, it was admitted by the Russian colonel, some torture, a large number of non-commissioned officers and men were executed. Hudson was extremely unhappy about the proceedings, but the British had always made it clear that they were in no way responsible for the discipline of the Russians who had their own code of law. The method of execution, too, must have been revolting, although he did not know it at the time. The firing party consisted of two Lewis machine guns fired at ground level. They could not aim higher than at their victims' legs.

When Hudson expostulated about Russian methods, the Russian colonel replied bitterly: 'You British don't realise what we are up against. You come out here from comfortably secure homes, knowing full well you can return to them. For us, it's a good deal more than just our own individual life and death. The issue affects the whole of Russia.' He went on to explain the methods used by the Bolsheviks in their bid to take over Russia and, he said, the world. Hudson was silenced.

At Force Headquarters there was a sprinkling of British officers and among them a young intelligence officer. He had fallen in love with a very beautiful Russian nurse in the hospital, a Baltic baroness. Her father had been shot by the Bolsheviks.

After the failed mutiny, Hudson was sitting in his railway carriage office when a clerk announced that the baroness was outside asking for an interview on a matter of urgent importance. He was entirely taken aback when she indignantly told him that the Russian commanding officer of the hospital had refused her permission to witness the executions of the mutineers and she wanted the general to overrule him.

Nothing I could say would shake her determination. She became almost hysterical and stormed at me. Ever since she had seen her own father shot, she had sworn to be present at the shooting of some Bolsheviks. She could never be at peace until she had. As she raved on I saw through the window behind her a party of dejected-looking prisoners surrounded by armed guards being marched down the platform and I realised that if I could keep her talking a little longer she would be too late. In the hope of pacifying her, I told her the General was out but I would see what I could do. Then I sat down and wasted time in writing a note to her Commanding Officer. In it I said, if he could detain her a little longer, the executions would be over. I was told later that as soon as he had released her, she had run nearly a mile, round by a circuitous route, to avoid the guards surrounding the place of execution and though too late to see the shooting, she had insisted on being shown the horribly mutilated bodies before they were buried. To me it seemed almost impossible to believe that this educated, and in every other way apparently well-balanced and refined girl, could have been capable of this. I had yet a lot to learn.

Russians are born intriguers, and the atmosphere in which we lived was especially conducive to intrigue. It was almost impossible to talk for any time to any educated Russian without becoming acutely conscious of the tragedy in his personal life. All were cut off from their homes and few, if any, had escaped without the loss by violence of some at least of their nearest relatives. Amongst the White Russians those officers belonging to the upper classes mainly adopted the attitude of eat, drink and be merry for tomorrow we die, but in fact they could only hope to be merry under the influence of drink. At all other times they were obsessed with suspicion both of each other and in particular of those who had risen through the ranks, whom they knew had a chance of rehabilitation in their own country if they were to bow the knee to Communism. No officer could entirely trust his men, for all knew that there were many Bolshevik agents in the ranks, busily engaged in anti-White Russian propaganda. This in itself was terribly unsettling. Apart from the now familiar ideological appeal, the propagandists pointed to the withdrawal of the French troops, followed later by the Americans and set it about that the British intended to seize and hold North Russia for good. Alternatively they asked, what exactly was the White Russian policy? Was it to set up another tsarist regime? As no two White Russian leaders could agree on any clear-cut answer to this question, the Red propagandists had it all their own way. They offered peace, the Whites an endless civil war. The men were told they were fighting either for the British against their own countrymen, or for some puppet counterfeit Tsar to be set up by the British in the teeth of public opinion. No man likes to be told he is a traitor to his country, a supporter of foreign usurpers.

There was something very childlike and confiding in the Russian soldiery in spite of all this, and I used to enjoy visiting them in their blockhouses. The men were not in the least subservient and laughed at the simplest sally. They were easily pleased by any word of praise, and were delighted to show their skill, which was considerable, in the building of their defences. I admired their extreme hardiness and cheerfulness in the bitter conditions of the front line.

Colonel Thornhill, the Chief Intelligence Officer on the Archangel front who had befriended me at Murmansk, visited us in connection with negotiations over an exchange of prisoners between ourselves and the Bolsheviks. He was to meet a small party from the other side, in no man's land, and I asked if I could accompany him.

At the appointed hour we marched out from our foremost post on the railway, preceded by a soldier carrying a large white flag. On reaching what we judged to be about half-way we halted and awaited the negotiators. We received no reply to our shouted enquiries and so we began to walk slowly forward. As we approached, it was evident there was great excitement in the enemy lines for soldiers were seen scurrying about. In spite of shouts of remonstrance we continued walking until we could conduct a conversation without having to shout. At long last three negotiators appeared. The understanding had been that we were all to be unarmed. I could not of course understand the conversation and, while they were busily employed, I stepped discreetly into the background hoping to get a photograph. One of the Bolsheviks turned round, saw me with the camera in my hand, and immediately drew a revolver. At this Thornhill let drive such a volley of imprecations that he soon had the Russians in complete and almost subservient control.

They had brought with them enlarged photographs of mutilated hands and feet belonging, they declared, to prisoners who had escaped from the White Russians and had been tortured while prisoners of war. On examination, these photos showed in at least one or two cases the stamp of the RAF photographic section which had been clumsily erased. When this was pointed out to them they hastily withdrew the photos, which were in fact photos of tortured men sent to the Bolsheviks by the White Russians on a South Russian front as proof of the fact that White Russian prisoners had been tortured. Thornhill told me later that he was certain the Reds had never had the slightest intention of arranging exchanges but they wanted the onus of refusal to rest with us.

Orders were received in early August 1919 for the total evacuation from North Russia of all British and other allied servicemen. The plan was for an attack to take place in order to cover the withdrawal. British troops were to take part, only in the opening phase, the Russians were then to take over. It was hoped that the Russian Government of the North would be firmly established. However, virtually nobody in touch with the reality of the situation believed this.

Some recently arrived RAF pilots had brought with them first-class photographic apparatus and I took the opportunity to get them to take photographs of the track running south from our outpost village of Bolshie Ozerki, which was not shown on any map we had. The photos showed that the track came out near a large railway bridge, and I asked the General if he would let me lead a mounted raid down this track, with the object of blowing up the bridge so that the Bolsheviks could not support their forward troops by railing forward reinforcements when we attacked.

He took some persuading but eventually he agreed and I set about collecting a party to carry out the scheme. Our Russian Prince, who combined the duties of interpreter and troop leader of our sixteen cavalrymen, was enthusiastic and offered to recruit a number of gunners who could ride to be used as mounted infantrymen and the necessary engineers. I impressed upon him that the whole party must be volunteers but must not be told the route or objective until we were well on our way. My plan was to spend the first night at Bolshie Ozerki, a short ride, but enough to get the party settled down. The British liaison officer at the village, a Northumberland Fusilier by name of Hutchinson, was very astonished to see us ride in and very keen to accompany us and as I had two Irish horses I agreed to him using one. The cavalrymen were mounted on troop horses and the rest on shaggy little Russian ponies. The gunners insisted on carrying enormous cavalry sabres in addition to their rifles, a ludicrous sight for the sabres almost reached the ground. Our gear, reduced to a minimum, was carried on pack ponies as we had two bridgeless rivers to cross.

We started well before dawn with the cavalry, the Prince and myself in the advance guard and Hutchinson at the head of the main body, in all fifty or sixty men. The first river presented no obstacle but it was getting late by the time we reached the second and we decided to camp on the near bank and tackle the crossing, which looked formidable, the following morning.

The passage of the river next day gave our Cossacks an opportunity of exhibiting their skill in standing on their saddles as their horses half waded, half swam, across. I got my legs wet. The stores had to be floated across on improvised rafts and the ponies persuaded to swim.

I was riding with the Prince, his sergeant major and a dozen men behind us, when suddenly the two scouts ahead of us came galloping back and almost at the same moment a burst of machine gun fire zipped through the trees high above our heads. The Prince, ever impetuous, wanted to charge, but I pulled my horse across the path and told him to find out from the scouts first if there was wire ahead. The fire stopped after the first burst and a gong was furiously beaten. The scouts said there was a barricade across the track. It was an old woman gathering sticks who had raised the alarm. They had seen a big lake in the forest behind the barricade with a lot of soldiers bathing or rowing about in boats. They had only seen one sentry at the barricade but he had a machine gun. It seemed obvious that if we could get round the flank of the barricade in time we could win the day but the horses, of which mine was the worst offender, were plunging about, frightened by the fire.

Perhaps unwisely, I decided to dismount. I had just told the Prince to come with me and six men when Hutchinson arrived.

He had come on alone to see what was happening. I told him to bring forward all the riflemen he could and I would send back to the track for them. A short detour through the forest enabled us to see that the barricade was only a short one and had no wire round the sides. This was good enough. If we could get the main body up in time we could overrun the garrison before they were ready for us, for judging from the shouting they were in panic. Leaving our few men to watch, the Prince and I started running back to the track to bring them up. What with horse-holders and engineers we were reduced to about thirty men all told and as the Prince addressed them I got the impression that they were far from enthusiastic. It dawned on me that many of them were deliberately holding back. The forest, though clear of undergrowth, was fairly thick; I had edged my way well out to the left when I saw three enemy tip-toeing through the trees to my right and about 40yd away. The man nearest me made a warning gesture with his hand as the other two dropped down, then he went down on one knee behind a tree and slowly raised his rifle. I saw that Hutchinson, quite oblivious of his danger, was the target. I fired wildly very approximately in his direction a fraction of a second before he fired.

Very quietly I drew back and started running with pounding heart round to where Hutchinson was, praying he had not been hit. At my shot a lot of fire was opened up from the barricade but it was all well above our heads. I found Hutchinson unhurt but he told me the Russians had all run back and the Prince had gone back to rally them. The Prince began to address them. A man stood out and spoke. He said they were not cowards and that they would have been ready to follow their officers anywhere if proper arrangements had been made for dealing with the wounded but, as it was, what chance had a wounded man of getting back alive? We had not even got a doctor with our party.

'We've got medical panniers and two trained dressers,' the Prince whispered.

'Tell them that,' I said, 'and tell them that when they get back everyone will know as well as we do that it's only an excuse for running away.'

As the Prince finished his translation, outcry and argument broke out and it was obvious that by now our hope of success was shattered and I told the Prince to give the orders for an ignominious withdrawal, his Cossacks now acting as a rearguard.

An incident occurred on the way back which shows how easily panic can break out among demoralised men. Just as we ourselves were about to get mounted, a capercaillie, a great heavy bird, came silently flapping over our heads. The Sergeant Major automatically raised his rifle and I said, 'Go on, shoot, I bet you don't hit it.' The Sergeant Major fired and the bird heeled over but flew off unscathed.

Failing to catch the party up at a trot we broke into a canter but still failed. I began to let my horse out and was really galloping when I heard shots ahead. Coming round a bend I found myself in full pursuit of our own men. When we managed to bring them to a halt they said they had been attacked from the rear. The Sergeant Major's single shot had grown into a hail of fire from which only by the skin of their teeth had they escaped. Thus, ingloriously, ended our raid behind the enemy lines, but realised that this was largely due to faulty preparation. I had left too much to the Prince who like most Russians of the old Tsarist days expected blind obedience without understanding. I doubt very much if the men were really volunteers. On the whole we were lucky the raid did not end in a disaster.

The attack on the railway was a great success. The Australians met little resistance, and the Russians then took over.

On about 10 September Hudson's brigade headquarters embarked on a train at Obozerskaya en route to Archangel where they were destined to board a ship to return to Britain. In full uniform on the platform stood the commanding officer of the White Russian battalion, which had nearly mutinied and with whom Hudson had become very friendly. This, in spite of his dismissive attitudes towards the normal tenets of military law, Russian or British. As the train drew out, he shot himself.

Hudson's ship called in at Lerwick in the Shetland Islands. He left her there and found his own way home.

> I had gone out to Russia intending to find out what I could about Bolshevism, and on return I tried to sum up in my mind what I had learnt. The conclusion I came to, which did not alter much after, was that the regime based on absolute materialism, supported by force and ruthless cruelty, could not survive indefinitely. But to overcome such a regime two things were needed: first, a positive appeal; second, a leader who could inspire the people with an abiding faith in the Cause which they could understand.
>
> The White Russians had no appeal, other than a blind hatred of their opponents, and, having none, no leader could arise who could weld opposition to the existing evil regime into successful action.
>
> When asked how long I thought it would be before the necessary conditions were forthcoming, I suggested ten or twelve years. I did not understand then the inherent strength of a Police State. *(These words were written long before the dismantling of the Soviet Empire.)*

At this stage it may well be opportune to examine Hudson's motivations during his remarkable military career in the First World War. His conventional social background of the country gentry in England at the turn of the century no doubt was a major factor in his state of mind during the many actions in which he was involved. But he certainly was no military automaton. He thought for himself and had a broad range of literary interests. His poems, some of which appear in this book, speak for themselves. He searched for beauty, and truth often touched with humour in almost any situation. He was not a rebel in the sense of broadening his perception of the futility of war into an active campaign against it, as, at one stage of his turbulent life, did Siegfried Sassoon. He accepted situations as they were and did his best in the circumstances to improve matters whatever the personal risk he might incur, and that was often very considerable. On the other hand, he had little respect for authority, particularly if he thought it was exercised in a thoughtless or stultifying manner. Throughout his career, and this will again become clear later on in this book, he was prepared to disregard orders if it seemed to him at the time to be right to do so. Perhaps the most remarkable instance of this came when he personally cut the line to battalion headquarters in order to make an unauthorised attack, which in the event was highly successful (page 90).

As already stated, his social background although in no way prompting his tendency to rebellion against existing authority and disobeying orders – very much the opposite – undoubtedly was a factor in his capacity for leadership. It also contributed to his almost fanatical regard for honesty in all aspects. He was brought up in a deferential world where status was accepted as an unquestioned fact of life. As far as he was concerned there was no question of letting down those who found themselves, however temporarily or irrationally, under his command. As has already been pointed out, this did not necessarily apply to his dealing with his superiors.

Again and again, however, one is forced to conclude that the most formative incident of his life came at his preparatory school when he was unmercifully bullied by a sadistic headmaster. Here was born Hudson's disregard for authority and his capacity to overcome physical stress in all its forms: if he could survive the regular nightly ordeals at the hands of his tormentor he could survive anything. His self-confidence – and throughout his life this was a prominent but non-arrogant feature of his character – stemmed in part from his success in overcoming physical stress at his public school. It also came about from the realisation that he was not, as he had repeatedly been told, stupid. The world, with all its problems, complexities and delights was opened up for him by his schoolmaster at Sherborne, Trevor Dennis.

Hudson's motivation was, at least in part, a determination to prove himself not so much to others as to himself. It was a personal struggle, which he was determined to win again and again. And he did.

A further element in Hudson's motivation was his deep love for his country. Whatever happened he was not going to let his country down. Nowadays patriotism is widely held to be incorrect, politically and in every other way. Instant communication has shrunk the world and devotion to one small part of it appears irrational, selfish and petty. It was not so in the early twentieth century. There was an immense, and justified, pride in the creation of the British Empire with all its faults and glories. This almost unbelievable creation by the peoples of a small offshore island was seen as a colossal, almost sublime, achievement.

Throughout his life, and particularly during the First War when death was highly likely, Hudson thought a great deal about the eternal questions of a possible afterlife and the existence of a beneficent God. As a very young man he had been impressed by the Buddhist monk he met in Ceylon and in his unquestioning acceptance of the transmigration of souls. Brought up in an all-pervading acceptance of Protestant Christian belief in all its aspects, he came to be very doubtful about some of the assertions it made. As far as the war was concerned, he did not see it as a personal crusade against evil. He was doubtful about all the certainties which pervaded much of government inspired propaganda. His doubts had extended to the many instances of premonition he had seen in some of his fellow officers. Sometimes these turned out to be true and death had indeed followed a premonition of that disaster, but sometimes it had not. On one occasion, just before the action in which he won his Victoria Cross, his premonition of personal disaster had been well founded. This led him to reflect on his attitude to the Almighty.

With an attack pending, it was natural that I should be nervous, but there was a certainty of impending personal disaster in my mind, which was quite different in kind from any previous experience. Whether the outcome was to be death or not seemed curiously unimportant. In a way I find my feelings difficult to explain. I was not fighting fear. I was struggling with myself for strength to accept anticipated physical pain, and overcoming it by something greater, which I knew existed though I was unable to define it. It was a very real experience.

When at last I rose and made my way back to Headquarters, my mind was at rest. To say that I had prayed, and that comfort had resulted, would be the easy explanation, but I knew the truth was not as simple as that. My faith in God had remained as uncertain as ever it was throughout my struggle. I had not just submitted my will to God. I did not believe that a thinking man could evade his own responsibility so easily. A child does not overcome his childish difficulties or fears merely by calling on his parents for help, however loving and willing to help they may be. Almost immediately after infancy, a child is conscious of his own individuality, and knows he must fight his own battles in matters other than purely material ones. Consciousness of free will is one of the first experiences of life. It is only later that attempts are sometimes made to refuse to accept the reality of free will and personal responsibility.

Again and again when one examines Hudson's motivations one comes up against the fact that, although he was inevitably largely a product of his background in all its aspects, political and religious, he thought for himself. He made his own decisions on the basis of his own personal beliefs. He was his own man.

SEVEN

• • • • • • • • • •

Peace

The Metamorphosis of Thomas Fish

An aged man was pottering
Along a winding lane
With short slow steps
And many stops
With groans and grumbles grizzling.

A little boy was loitering
Towards him down the lane
With short brisk steps
But many stops
To poke and pry aplundering.

They met at a corner meandering
Along the winding lane.
The boy was scared,
The old man stared,
And I could see him puzzling.

Said white beard to the foundling
'I know you, what's your name?'

'Sir, an you wish,
It's Thomas Fish.'
'That's mine,' said the old man grumbling.

On his return from Russia, Hudson married. His wife, Gladys Lee, had come from Allendale in Northumberland: her family had farmed there for several centuries, as designated in the local church register moving up the social scale from 'farmer' (a farmer employed nobody) to 'yeoman' (a yeoman employed somebody) to 'gentleman' when coal was found under their land. Work; less work; no work! She had been his nurse on his arrival in the London Hospital after being wounded in Italy. They had been engaged but had broken it off, hence one of his reasons for the foray into Russia. In any event, they came together again and 'lived happily ever after'. He was deeply in love with her for the rest of his life. He was, however, plunged into a quandary – what was he to do with the rest of his life? He had no money of his own apart from his meagre Army pay as a captain (marriage allowances were not paid until the recipient reached the age of 30) and his wife had a very small allowance. His decision to stay in the Army was reached in the main because he saw no possibility of earning his living in any other way. He was no military enthusiast at that stage of his life.

After a period as second-in-command of a company he was made adjutant to the regimental depot in Derby. With no money to spare the young couple had to live very frugally – they could rarely afford to go to 'the pictures' for instance. They managed to buy a car, which had to be unloaded before it went up a hill. There was no driving test in those days and Hudson had several hilarious confrontations, including hitting a bread van in Piccadilly and the bread being scattered all over the road.

His life was full of contrasts. Perhaps the most ludicrous was when he was sent on a rifle course at the School of Musketry at Hythe. Having commanded a battalion for two years in war in the most challenging circumstances, the Army sent him to learn about the Lee Enfield rifle, extraction and so on. It is not surprising that, however well intentioned the instructor, Hudson found it difficult to take the course seriously.

The young couple were living in Derby in a most dreary semi-detached red brick house in a long and grimy street on a tram route. They lived on Army rations: 'Tough frozen meat, stodgy, badly baked bread, margarine and rat-trap cheese.' To add to their miseries their first child died in childbirth – in fact unnecessarily because the local doctor had failed to make a proper examination before the arrival of the baby. The two subsequent sons born in 1922 and 1925 were Caesarean births. The deep joy of their arrival is reflected in two of Hudson's poems.

Mother Love

No-one
Has got such a wonderful, wonderful, baby
As we
Though why it should be
You must not ask me
It took us all three
The baby and Daddy and me
To make such a wonderful baby
No-one
Has got such a wonderful, wonderful, baby

No-one
Has got such a wonderful, wonderful, baby
You see
The best things are free
A flower or a tree
The limitless sea
And now you, his Daddy, and me

Have got our wonderful baby.
No-one
Has got such a wonderful, wonderful, baby

Mummy

Patter, patter tiny feet
Sturdy legs and toes so neat.
'I will catch you, if I can,
My beloved little man.'

Running, laughing, full of glee,
Shouting loudly, 'Can't catch me.'
When he's caught she'll hold him tight,
Kiss him breathless with delight.

When he tumbles, 'It's just fun,
My beloved little one,
Keep that quivering lip held tight,
Fight back tears with all your might.'

His adored sister Dolly had married Phillip Jelf who was in the Colonial Service in Northern Rhodesia (now Zambia). In January 1923 Jelf was a District Commissioner at Luwingu, 100 miles away on dirt roads from the nearest doctor. He was woken up at 3 a.m. by a lion which had jumped through his window, was lying on top of him and was trying to eat him! He struggled clear and, as he put it:

I crashed about the room, dodging round furniture and eventually through the dressing-room archway where I collapsed on the floor, face down, while the lion lay on top of me chewing my right shoulder. Then I heard a shot fired and the lion left me.

I had just enough strength left to get up, open the door and stagger to the store room where I locked myself in.

A companion staying in the bungalow had summoned armed assistance from the local jail. Shots had been fired, one of which lodged in Jelf's body. After a pain-wracked journey he returned to England. He never fully recovered from the attack.

Life in the Regular Army in the 1920s was not exhilarating, to say the least. After Derby, Hudson was sent to Northern Ireland. He always seemed to get something wrong. He forgot the annual regimental inspection and turned up in his workaday Army uniform to the huge annoyance of the inspecting officer. He lost his temper with a general who with his staff was standing over a soldier as he attempted to shoot on the range. The soldier was managing only to hit a few stones in front of him when the general made some unpleasant remark.

Hudson said to the general: 'I don't know how you expect this wretched man to shoot properly in front of a whole crowd of brass hats. He is just petrified.' Not surprisingly, Hudson's stock as a peacetime soldier waned considerably as time went on. He failed the Staff College exam twice, the first time through illness, but at last he succeeded and received a vacancy at Camberley. Hudson was nothing if not self-critical. He summed up his two years as a student at the Staff College:

> For the first time I found myself in close contact with a number of officers of my own age and standing, and this in itself was invaluable experience. Almost against my will, I became so afraid of appearing to curry favour with my instructors that as time went on I went to the other extreme, and became abnormally stubborn and argumentative. I had, in any case, a fixed idea that the last war had been shamefully mismanaged, nor did it seem to me that the teaching then given at the Staff College would be likely to make any future war less mercilessly blood-thirsty. Had they taken me seriously, my attitude must have been irritating to

both my instructors and my fellow students. By the end of my two years as a student, the Staff had pretty accurately summed me up as inclined to be awkward and pig-headed, but not really aggressively-minded. Officially, this was put in more formal phraseology in my final report, but I was given quite a good recommendation as regards further employment in the Army. . . .

The staff and students of my time included four future field marshals and a number of high-ranking generals. Of the future field marshals, my first commandant, General Ironside, I had known in Russia; another, General Wilson, I saw very little of, as he was not directly concerned with my year. Of the other two, Montgomery was on the staff as an instructor and Alexander was a fellow student, though senior in rank to Monty. With the aid of a quick promotion in the Irish Guards he was then a full Colonel.

An outstanding memory of Monty was of his sitting firmly on the fireguard in the mess, the centre of a number of the students, affirming that the weakness in modern generals lay in their inability to make a personal impact on their men, owing to the size of modern armies. 'When I am a General,' he said, 'I shall adopt some distinctive mark, possibly some unusual form of dress, by which I shall be known to every private in my army.' [Author's note – hence Monty's Tank Corps beret, with two badges.]

Hudson went on to describe Alexander, Montgomery's future rival and boss:

Even Alexander, the most apparently unself-advertising of men, had personal idiosyncrasies which drew attention. His boyish delight in physical agility, his neatness with pen and pencil, his German upturned uniform caps, his tunics of unusual material, his trick of using his eyebrows to denote either amused surprise or friendliness or frosty disapproval, all these differentiated him from his fellow men in any company.

Monty arrived at a conclusion through hard thought and severely logical reasoning; Alexander, with a swift realisation of basic principles, accepted or refused the opinions of others whom he consulted with an open mind.

After the first year at the Staff College, Hudson was warned that he risked being dropped from the course. He was told that he was either lacking in interest or being consistently lazy.

In fact my only consistency was rebellion against the methods preached by my instructors. They seemed to me to differ little, if at all, from those which failed, as I saw it, in the last war. It was always the same dawn attack with lines of infantrymen following behind the bombardment, and a sprinkling of tanks to resuscitate the advance when the infantry had been, as it was euphemistically put, held up by fire.

As Hudson saw it, if the Army was to fight in Europe, a predominantly armoured organisation was required, supported by a trained parachute force to land behind the enemy defences. On the other hand the need in India and other outposts of Empire was for infantry trained to act in aid of the civil power. In his view, training at the Staff College fell hopelessly between these two stools and he consistently said so. He was lucky to survive.

Like many young men of his ilk, during the General Strike he joined enthusiastically in trying to sustain some kind of order. His task was to help in the distribution of the Government magazine, the *British Gazette*.

One day, outside the office on the Embankment in London, he saw 'an old bearded sandwich-man parading the pavement with boldly-printed notices adjuring the public "To hang Locker Lampson from the nearest lamppost"' (Lampson, an MP, was one of the leading figures in the anti-General Strike movement).

Late one evening, on returning to the offices, I was astonished to recognise the old man sitting on the floor in the passage outside the secretary's door. I demanded to know what he was doing. He said he had come for his pay! At this moment the door onto the passage opened and, looking rather embarrassed, Locker Lampson's secretary hailed him in. This was a form of publicity that was new to me, and an eye-opener into the wiles of publicity managers.

After the Staff College, Hudson returned to Northern Ireland with his regiment for six months before being sent to Singapore for his first staff appointment as staff officer to the local forces on the island, the equivalent to the Territorials in England. This led to a most unfortunate, not to say tragic, development for his family. The conventional wisdom was that the elder son, John, aged 8, was too old to go to the climate of Singapore. If he did so, it was said, his health would be irrevocably damaged. The author, as the younger son, aged only 4½, was deemed able to accompany his parents without danger. The upshot was that John was left behind while the author went with his parents. It was an impossible situation for John who felt very bitter about it, not understanding or accepting the reasoning. It was a most difficult choice for Hudson and his wife and they always bitterly regretted it. Nowadays no such distinction is made, quite rightly and, in any case, the aeroplane has made it much easier to keep families together.

During the otherwise halcyon days of the British Raj this division of families, often with all the children being left behind while their parents went to India or elsewhere, must have had a devastating psychological effect on tens of thousands of Britons.

On his return from Singapore in 1932, Hudson joined a new regiment, the King's Own Scottish Borderers (KOSB). He had been told that there was a complete blockage of promotion in the Sherwood Foresters and that he would be most unlikely ever to command a battalion as by the time he was top of the list he would be too old. On the other hand he would command the KOSB shortly. His first appointment in his new regiment was as second-in-command to a battalion at Fort George near Inverness.

He was there for six months. He had a somewhat frosty reception as his new commanding officer probably resented him for, as he saw it, making use of his regiment for personal advantage. This attitude did not last long, in spite of Hudson, as always, upsetting some of his colonel's practice manoeuvres by making idiosyncratic decisions when acting as 'enemy'. Furthermore, as a result of the existing Army practice of 'brevet' rank, Hudson found himself senior to his commanding officer when acting as garrison commander. They both had to request leave from each other.

Hudson's next appointment was in 1933 as Chief Instructor at the Royal Military College at Sandhurst where he spent four happy years with his family in the comparative luxury of a large Army quarter. A distant relative through his mother, Lord MacKenzie (a Law Lord), came to his financial rescue and the family had many most enjoyable fishing holidays at a house on Loch Maree near Poolewe in north-west Scotland. The comparative turbulence of the past seemed to be subsiding.

Hudson rejoined the KOSB, again as second-in-command, at Catterick in Yorkshire. From there they were sent to Portsmouth where Montgomery was their boss as their brigadier. The German military attaché was visiting the regiment and Monty, to Hudson's great astonishment, told him that the British people would never fight for the rights of a remote and unknown people such as the Czechs and that there was no danger of a second world war over such an issue. Next day they happened to go for a walk alone together along the front.

Perhaps foolishly I remarked what a dangerous statement he had made the night before. Very angry, he inquired what right I had to criticise. Hoping to appease him by the implied compliment I said that a rising soldier, such as he was, would be sure to have his own dossier in the German intelligence records and that any remark of that sort coming from him would undoubtedly be reported. The Germans had gone into the First War to some extent because they thought the British would not join in, and we did not want history to repeat itself. Nevertheless our walk was brought to an abrupt conclusion and I knew I had offended him deeply.

There then occurred one of the most abrupt changes of fortune in a life which, it must be said, was rarely without surprises. Hudson had just been told that he was to command a battalion of the KOSB, then in India, when he was informed that he was promoted to the rank of brigadier to command the 2nd Infantry Brigade of the 1st Infantry Division then at Aldershot. This formation was clearly destined to go to France as part of the British Expeditionary Force in the event of war with Germany. Hudson's promotion to such an elite position over the heads of all the existing commanding officers in the British Army was astonishing. In many minds it was linked to the Secretary of State for War, Hore Belisha, whom he had met when directing a tattoo in Leeds and who had clearly been impressed. Furthermore, Hore Belisha had just promoted General Lord Gort to be Chief of the Imperial General Staff over the heads of several more senior generals including General Dill, then Commander-in-Chief in Aldershot. Gort also had a Victoria Cross and the natural conclusion was that Hudson's promotion before he had even commanded a battalion in peacetime was due to the same influence.

The situation was extremely embarrassing. Montgomery told Hudson's commanding officer that in his opinion the appointment was a shocking one since he had far too little experience to justify taking over a brigade in the Expeditionary Force. Hudson seriously considered refusing the appointment, 'But after some thought I came to the conclusion that I should have a go at it. Having come to this decision I went off with my family for a fortnight's skiing holiday.' Not surprisingly, the press got hold of the story and cuttings from *The Times*, the *Star*, the *Natal Mercury* and the *Malay Mail* can be seen in Appendix C.

Hudson's propensity for offending officers senior to him was never more in evidence than in the following two years. The commander of the division of which his brigade was a part was General Alexander and the Commander-in-Chief was General Dill. His first encounter with this latter august figure was when he was half-an-hour late for an official dinner and, on arrival, found everyone waiting for him and his wife (who had mistaken the time of the invitation). Then, on a training exercise, Dill arrived to find the vehicles of Hudson's brigade parked in rows on a road. This was in fact in the operation instructions in order to avoid damage to farmland. Refusing to listen to any explanation Dill left the scene, clearly in a fury. Misunderstandings of that nature seemed to continue throughout Hudson's stay in Aldershot. Without ever actually breaking the ground rules set for an exercise, he would never follow the expected course of action, making his own decisions and frequently confusing umpires and generals alike by arriving with his Brigade at an unexpected place and time. His original meeting with his divisional commander, Alexander, was a frosty affair, probably because of suspicions Alexander might have had of how he had obtained his position, but this situation improved and Alexander was able to save Hudson when Dill wrote an adverse annual report on Hudson's capabilities.

The outbreak of war with Germany was fast approaching and Hudson was amazed that, in the last manoeuvre in which he took part before war started, he should have had a German officer assigned to him.

Such was his keenness that he actually joined my HQ at two o'clock in the morning. We were engaged in a river crossing, and I was just going down to a portion of my front where a successful crossing had been made and where the engineers were building a bridge. I took him along in my jeep. It was just getting light when the bridge was completed. The infantry had crossed some time before in boats and as I could get no news of where they had got to I motored over the bridge to find out. Some of our men directed me down a track through a wood saying they thought their battalion headquarters had gone that way. As we rounded a corner, I saw General Dill standing quietly on the side of the track with two or three staff officers and at almost the same moment I saw the 'enemy'. We were within about 30 yards of them. The 'enemy' wore soft hats and we were in steel helmets. They had only to open fire and an umpire would have put us out of action. Presumably they thought that being in a vehicle we were something to do with a General and they did nothing. The driver had seen them, too, and quickly getting into reverse, he backed down the track and out of sight. By a lucky chance I and my German had escaped an ignominious capture under the eyes of the C-in-C who at a subsequent conference remarked that he did not wish to discourage commanders from being well forward in the battle, but there were reasonable limits!

The German was very surprised that he was allowed to examine any weapons we had and see what he liked. He hinted on many occasions that we must have some secret weapons which we were hiding from him. I told him that I wished we had, but he obviously did not believe me. He openly derided our anti-tank rifle, which he said would certainly not pierce German armour but did not mention that, at that time, the Germans had little armour to pierce.

On returning later to Aldershot, I drove him in my private car to the hotel in which he was being housed. Leaving my car near the door, I took him in and gave him a drink. When I came out a policeman met me and pointed out that I had parked the car on the wrong side of the road. I do not think anything he saw in England astonished my German more that the fact that a civilian policeman had the temerity to challenge the right of a senior

British officer to park his car where he liked. His opinion of the British Army up to that moment fairly high, dropped to zero.

War was now upon us and with a heavy heart I at last realised that it was inevitable. To cling on to the hope of a last moment reprieve was just wishful thinking. I said goodbye to my German, in the full knowledge that the next time we met, if we did, it would be our mutual duty to shoot each other!

EIGHT

• • • • • • • • • • •

Second World War Dunkirk

Orders for the mobilisation of the Army came through on 1 September 1939. Hudson went to France with his brigade, which consisted of three battalions – the North Staffordshire, the Gordon Highlanders and the Loyals, and they found themselves in an extension of the famous Maginot Line. Their anti-tank guns did not fit into the French pillboxes and they had to borrow French guns and ammunition – an extra complication to an already complicated situation. Eventually it became clear that there were three possibilities: to remain where they were and allow the Germans to march through Belgium without hindrance; to advance into Belgium to support the Belgian Army, possibly right up to their far border; or to advance to the River Dyle, 15 miles beyond Brussels, in order to hold positions which the Belgians were said to have prepared. The Belgians were terrified of not being entirely neutral and no reconnaissance of the positions was allowed. It was even very difficult to get maps.

Attached to my Headquarters were three French liaison officers and they represented very clearly three attitudes of mind. One was a university professor. He, I was told, was communist in leaning, though I thought it would be truer to say of him that he was merely anti-fascist. The second was a cheerful, good-natured bourgeois whose main concern was making the most of the present by finding as quickly as possible the best-looking girl in any village where we happened to be. The third was a serious-minded young royalist. One might say that the mind of the first centred on France, the second on Paris, the third on the French Empire as a whole.

The day before Armistice Day I received an invitation from the chairman of the committee of old soldiers of our small town to lay a wreath at 11 a.m. at the town war memorial. This I was about to accept when the university professor warned me to be careful. He then explained that in the town were two opposing sections of the community, and that the Mayor's invitation would shortly arrive, requesting me to lay a wreath at the memorial at 12 noon. It appeared that there were two factions in the town bitterly opposed to one another. What exactly the quarrel between the factions was I never gathered, but I now realise it was largely between the fascists and the communists. My first inclination was to accept the Mayor's invitation, as he was the official head of the town, but I was told that it happened he was also the leader of one faction and by doing so I would appear to be in sympathy with his particular party. In the end I took my own line and said, I hope politely, but quite firmly, that I would only attend any ceremony if both parties were present at the same time.

This ultimatum was accepted, and at the memorial on the following day the two parties were lined up, glowering at each other. As soon as the ceremony was over the parties made for their particular café and I had to visit them both to drink their health. All this might have been amusing had we merely been observers, but, in fact, we were considerably more, for this divided France was our chief ally in the face of a German attack and, on land, very much the senior ally.

Before long we began to get visits from ENSA theatrical parties, led by some prominent professional entertainers. One of these was giving a show in Amiens and I asked them to lunch with us on a Sunday in a café in our town. Their bus arrived in the square just as the populace, in deep black, was coming out from mass. They stood on the steps of the church to watch the arrival in bewildered and shocked astonishment. I had reinforced my own staff with a number of young Gordon Highlander subalterns who were billeted nearby. The young ladies of the ENSA party appeared in bright blouses and tight trousers of every hue, the Gordon Highlanders in kilts. Never in the history of the town, in peace or war, had the townspeople seen women in trousers and men in skirts. Like typical Englishmen we were inclined to take pride in foreigners thinking us mad; in practice they thought us uncouth.

Hudson's brigade was training on the Somme when, on 10 May 1940, Hitler's armies attacked Belgium. It was decided to take the third option: advance to the River Dyle in Belgium. Having returned to their original positions, the brigade had a six-and-a-half-hour transport lift along the crowded roads leading to the frontier. They passed through Brussels, one battalion becoming completely lost at night in the maze of backstreets. Some of the inhabitants of the city welcomed the British as their saviours but others, as it turned out correctly, expected the Germans to advance through Belgium without much trouble. They thought that, as in the First World War, their city would be occupied by the Germans again with all that implied. Hudson was billeted on a professor of the University of Brussels during the first night of the advance up to the Dyle.

He had recently lost his wife and was living with his two very attractive daughters. The professor had no illusions, either about the French or his own countrymen. He had been through the first war and had had no faith in the possibility of his country remaining neutral in a second war. During dinner he tried to maintain a reasonably cheerful view of the future but when the two girls withdrew he broke down. What chance, he said, had his daughters of coming through an inevitable occupation? Nothing he could say, he told me, would induce his daughters to leave the doomed city. The townspeople had not even been allowed to provide themselves with shelters from bombing or adequate black-out arrangements for fear of offending the Germans. The small British Army, gallant fighters as they might be, he said, were just walking into a trap. They would have to retire as certainly as they had had to withdraw from Mons in the first war. The Germans would then march in. I tried not to agree with him, but felt on uncomfortably insecure ground.

When they reached the frontage of the River Dyle assigned to Hudson's brigade it happened that a battalion of his old regiment, the Sherwood Foresters, was temporarily holding it. The handover went smoothly. The river itself was hardly more than a stream, but it was being dammed back in sections so that it would rise enough to make it more of a tank obstacle. However, this had not yet been done and it remained a minor obstacle to a major attack. Two bridges had been prepared for demolition.

As always, Hudson looked for positive, even aggressive solutions to military problems and he decided that the best defence would be to make a night attack on the German boats and transport that would have to be brought up. The timing of such an operation was clearly most important. A plan was worked out and the raiding party was briefed.

It was not long before refugees began to appear. A post was established on the road to give them water but there was nothing else that could be done to help them. Hudson describes the scene.

Watching the post one evening I saw family after family limping by, the strained white-faced, half-starved mother, the trail of tired children, the old granny perched perhaps with pathetic household goods on a ramshackle cart drawn by an underfed horse. Pushcarts, perambulators, stern-faced nuns in charge of an exhausted crocodile of children: all were struggling blindly on in the fond hope that Brussels, their capital city, would be able to give them food and shelter.

It was on the Dyle that I heard for the first time the almost continuous lowing of cattle that seemed the ominous background music of the whole subsequent retreat. Those who would normally have milked the cows had fled and the wretched animals were suffering the agony of over-full udders. My driver, a countryman, used to milk cows to save them pain whenever he could, as did many other country-bred soldiers.

The next day Hudson motored forward to get in touch with the commanding officer of the 12th Royal Lancers, Lieutenant Colonel Lumsden, whose regiment was providing a screen for the whole of the British Army. The news was bad. The enemy had broken through and the divisional cavalry, the 13th/18th Hussars, were withdrawing and would have to cross the bridge over the Dyle, which was being guarded by Hudson's brigade. When they had all crossed Hudson was to order the bridge to be blown. If the situation was unclear, however, Hudson was to use his own discretion. One troop of the Hussars was still missing when the Germans approached the scene and Hudson blew the bridge.

It proved to be only just in time, for as the order was given two enemy motorbikes and sidecars drove down the causeway at full speed, their machine guns blazing. The first jumped the causeway as our men opened fire, 20yds from the bridge, throwing the rider clear. The second was hit and burst into flames. A German officer, thrown into the water, put up his hands and began wading towards our men but his own compatriot opened fire on him from the far bank and killed him. A wounded NCO, probably the rider of the first bike, was brought in by our men after dark and, though severely wounded, and dying when he reached my headquarters, he continued to repeat 'Heil Hitler' in a weaker and weaker voice until he died. I could only admire these brave men. There were, of course, those, as always, who were prepared to dismiss their sublime courage as mere fanaticism, but had they been our men they would have been heroes.

During that afternoon an order was received from a whole division to withdraw that night because a major breakthrough on the French army front had occurred. Hudson asked for permission to carry out his raid but this was refused. The withdrawal began.

Hudson's brigade then began an almost continual withdrawal to Dunkirk. After one day's hard marching General Alexander arrived on the scene and told Hudson how serious the news was. Enemy columns were bypassing his brigade through the gap made by the breakthrough on the French front. The march would have to continue at once if they were not to be cut off. Very few men or officers had had any sleep, but they had to carry on through Brussels to the next defensible position on the River Senne.

The city of Brussels was panic-stricken. Thousands of people were trying to get into the station hoping to escape by train. Three elderly Englishwomen begged Hudson to help them escape on one of the Army lorries, but he had to refuse. Once civilians were allowed to travel with the soldiers there would be no limit and the Army would have ceased to be a fighting machine.

They spent the whole of 18 May on the River Senne and, though shelled, saw little of the enemy.

This was the first time since leaving the Dyle that I had been able to get four consecutive hours' sleep. We were then told to withdraw again. The men were nearing the limit of their endurance and it was an agony to see them plodding on, scarcely able to put one foot in front of the other. . . . Heartbreaking as it was, I was astonished at the cheerfulness and humour that still persisted as it always does when British troops are really up against it.

Their next line of defence was the River Dendre, which they reached just in time to prevent the enemy from encircling them. They were then told to withdraw again.

It is not possible to imagine a more unmilitary manoeuvre than the one that followed throughout that day. On the right of the road my three battalions and on the left the three battalions of the Guards Brigade; all our transports filled the centre of the road. Refugee petrol-less cars were being pitched into ditches and refugees in thousands pouring from side roads had to be stopped and turned back. Overhead, flocks of enemy planes were passing over. Very few of these actually attacked us, but the threat was continually apparent, and later we were to see the targets further down the road which they were bombing.

Eventually they met up with some troop carriers with a young major in charge. 'He confirmed that he had been ordered to pick us up and before he could say more I began cursing him for failure to carry out his orders. To my consternation he collapsed and burst into tears. He was deadbeat, and I felt remorseful at my display of ill temper.' They managed to go some way with these troop carriers before they had to start marching again. 'At one point a refugee column of carts had been caught on the road by enemy aircraft. The sight was so appalling that my intelligence officer who was with me and I nearly vomited.'

A little later in the withdrawal, Hudson organised a counter-attack to be undertaken by the North Staffordshire Regiment.

This was followed by a successful raid by the Loyal Regiment and the Gordons during which some enemy prisoners were captured. Hudson was pleased to note that they, too, seemed utterly exhausted. At last a little respite came when the brigade spent four comparatively quiet days in the town of Lannoy.

> While we were there, enemy aeroplanes dropped pamphlets, written in English, on us. These announced that we were surrounded, the Belgians had capitulated and that we had better surrender to prevent further casualties. This was the first we had heard of a Belgian surrender. The men thought this a bad attempt at a bluff, though in fact it was truer than we thought at the time. The houses in our area were still full of civilian women and children, and during the afternoon and next morning we used our transport to carry them back to comparative safety. . . . There were some pitiful scenes, but it was the best we could do for these poor people. They, of course, largely blamed us for bringing the war to their town.

The withdrawal, or retreat would be a better word, continued. The situation became more and more chaotic as a mass of vehicles jammed the roads, which were already full of refugees. At one stage, as the brigade was awaiting an anticipated German attack,

> a thunderstorm had been working up, and now as I was walking round studying the country and talking to the men, one of the heaviest downpours of rain I have ever known in Europe came down. This terrific storm, and the continuous heavy rain that followed, has been said to have saved the British Army at various points along the line of retreat. What effect it really had on the exhausted Germans I do not know, but the anticipated attack on my Brigade certainly never materialised.
>
> There are always those who are prepared to attribute results in war to supernatural phenomena. The Angels of Mons and the

Miracle of Dunkirk are cases in point. In fact, it is the continuing resolution of leaders, and led, which counts. Had the Germans been resolute enough to press on with their encirclement in spite of difficulties, they could have cut off our line of retreat. Had we had the resolution to fight our way through in spite of this, we still would have reached our objective, the coast. During the next few days I was to see many of every rank, up to and including General officers who had failed in resolution and who were obviously thinking or beginning to think more of their own personal safety, or chances of escape, than of holding out against the enemy.

The retreat continued.

My Staff Captain, who had gone ahead, had found as a Headquarters a farmhouse down a small side road. It had cover trenches near it, presumably dug by previous occupants. As it got light I directed my troops into various areas and, on arrival at the farmhouse, found to my delight a kindly hostess and her grown-up daughter had put some coffee on to boil. I was very cold and wet, and thankful to accept, when an air-raid warning was sounded. Looking out we saw about fifteen enemy aeroplanes flying over. They turned and, one after the other, began to peel off and dive-bomb us. The next ten minutes I and a few others spent in terror of our lives under the shelter of a haystack while bombs rained down. My shame was considerable when, on returning to the house, I found the two women had never left their kitchen. On our reappearance they presented us with cups of steaming coffee.

I asked them why they had not gone into one of the trenches and they shrugged their shoulders and said they could not spare the time. In any case, wherever they went, they might be hit and they might as well stay at least warm in the house.

On the 29 May (Hudson's forty-eighth birthday) Hudson was leading his brigade marching on foot which, as far as he was concerned, was becoming very painful, when he was summoned to divisional headquarters. Arriving on the back of a motorcycle, he was told to go ahead as fast as he could to organise a defence of the inner canal near Bray-les-Dunes and take command of any troops he found there. He had picked up an engineer sergeant and was riding on the back of his motorcycle at speed down an open stretch road towards Bray,

> when some British soldiers on the road held up their hands and shouted to us to stop. I told the Sergeant to disregard them, and then suddenly I realised we were approaching a bridge. As we shot by the horrified soldiers we saw the bridge had been blown. Sappers had filled in most of the gap with planks, but had left, or not yet put in, the centre ones. There was no time to pull up and the Sergeant instead accelerated. This was the first and only time I have ever leapt a gap on the back of a motorbike. The Sergeant and I cheered as we swept through the astonished sappers on the far side. It was a very exhilarating experience.

Alexander had told Hudson that Bray had been given to him as his divisional area and that no French troops would be allowed to occupy it – but French troops were swarming round the bridge. An unorganised rabble of British soldiers was clamouring to cross the canal. These were heavy gunners, Royal Army Service Corps drivers, Pay Corps clerks, bakers, etc. They were all corps and army troops who are to be found in the back blocks of an army. Eventually an ordered situation was established and Hudson's brigade was in position on the line of the canal, which ran parallel and about three-quarters of a mile from the sea.

After a very smelly night in a pigsty, Hudson was woken to be told to send a battalion to Bergues where the enemy were said to be breaking through the division. The only battalion available in Hudson's brigade was the Loyal Regiment which was totally exhausted. Hudson went to see Alexander who, by this time, had assumed command of the corps, and tried to have the order changed. Alexander, however, 'remained calm but said he had no other alternative but to send them'. In spite of their exhaustion, the Loyals marched to Bergues and established a holding position there. Hudson sent a message to the commanding officer, Lieutenant Colonel Sandie: 'Well done, John. If other blokes could do the sort of thing the Loyals have done, it wouldn't be necessary to ask the Loyals to do the things they do. . . . Tell them all how well I think they have done.' Hudson went to the Esplanade at Dunkirk to tell Alexander all was well.

> There I met many officers whom I had not seen for years, now in various staffs and commands. One after another found themselves without anything to do except bemoan their fate and that of the British Army. The defeatist attitude was infuriating. The talk was entirely confined to our chances of being evacuated and how soon. I still just could not or would not bring myself to believe that the whole British Army was going to scuttle out of France. Surely, I thought, the French would be able to make some sort of comeback now, as seemed almost certain, the Germans had outstripped their administrative follow-up.
>
> It was obvious that the rabble on the beaches, who had no fighting value and were merely an encumbrance, should be evacuated, but why could we not hold on at least as a thorn in the flesh to the German advance further into France? Could we not, after a rest, break out and rescue a great part of the valuable equipment we had left littering the roads? Would not our presence help in the submarine war? . . . In fact there was very little bombing or machine-gunning of the troops ashore that I heard or saw for the enemy bombers, rightly from their point of view, reserved their efforts, such as they were, more for the ships out at sea or just offshore. . . . I only went to see the beaches once. They were a depressing sight. Thousands of British soldiers, many unarmed (for quite a high proportion of line

communication soldiers were not then armed with rifles), blackened the foreshore. They were just waiting to be removed, and one had the feeling that they felt no shame that this was so.

Our splendid 1st Division sappers had cleverly constructed an improvised quay capable of receiving small boats. This was done by running lorries head-to-tail out to sea at low tide and planking a roadway along the top of the cabins. The calm sea was a mass of every sort of shipping and small boats were ploughing to and from the larger ones taking on men. Some men were wading out to sea to meet the boats.

Hudson was then told to embark his brigade from the mole (a long pier) at Dunkirk. The rest of the division were to stay on another day and embark the following night. 'A deep cloud of frustration, anger and depression came over me at the thought of slinking away in the night and leaving others to face the music. At least it would have been some consolation to have been the last to go.' He and his brigade set off to try to find the mole.

We had no large-scale map and we only saw one individual in our hunt for the harbour, a French civilian slinking along probably on the look-out for loot. We asked for the boats and he waved us vaguely on but was very uncommunicative.

As we were walking down a wharf inside the harbour area, we came on a jumble of driver-less ambulances. I heard someone tapping on the sides of one and we rushed to open the back. It was full of wounded, moaning and asking for water. Horrified we opened ambulance after ambulance. They all contained wounded men. We could find no one about, and we hurried on for help, angry at the callous desertion of their charges by the drivers and attendants.

We met a quartermaster of one of the battalions, himself searching for the mole, who said his battalion was at least an hour's march behind. The mole, which I discovered later was about a kilometre long, was jammed to capacity with sleeping officers and men. I was told the Naval officer in charge of the embarkation was at the far end of the mole. It seemed to take an age to thread my way over the sleeping forms of the soldiery, but near the end there was a gap in the mole over which a single plank had been placed and here I found a Naval sentry.

The Naval captain had heard about the wounded, but said he had just received a message that one of the three hospital ships had been sunk as it stood out waiting for the tide to enable it to get alongside. No more ships of any kind would come in for the troops until the tide rose and after this there would be very few hours of daylight left. His orders were to abandon daylight loading, owing to the heavy casualties already suffered in daylight from air attacks.

I suggested he should at least take the wounded, but he said that even if I could arrange to carry them up, which I said I would do, taking one stretcher meant leaving at least three unwounded men behind. The Army would have to decide this point. Returning, I found a Royal Army Medical Corps officer. He was only a regimental doctor who had himself brought his wounded in by ambulance but he said he had at last found a responsible RAMC officer who was in the process of trying to organise the care of the wounded in their ambulances. With this, though far from happy, I left him to it and returned to my own business of getting my own men ready to embark. I had found there were long gaps in the mole between units where the men had just dropped down and it was nearing daylight. My first job was to rouse and close up the queue.

Eventually, through the chaos, Hudson's brigade reached their objective.

At the end of the mole I stood and watched my battalions being hustled onboard. They were tightly packed on deck, shoulder to shoulder. The Naval officers refused to allow the men to keep their rifles owing to the delay in getting them down the rope ladders onto the decks. Our men were very angry and being made to stack the rifles they had carried mile after mile but my protests to the Naval embarkation officer only met with the statement that this was an Admiralty order. I myself, and my own headquarter officers and men, went aboard a Monitor. The Captain could not have been kinder. We had not been long out to sea when I noticed a lot of signalling from the Mole to the ship. I asked the Captain what all this was all about. The message, marked very urgent, was in code from the Admiralty and its decoding had caused a considerable flutter amongst the Monitor officers. It turned out that enquiries were being made as to whether we had Lord Gort's ADC on board, and, if so, whether he had the General's kit. Life, I felt, was already coming back to normal.

On arrival in England Hudson protested by telephone to the War Office that his men were being ordered to leave their arms in France. He was told the order had been cancelled more than once already but they would try again. He was told that the train he was about to join at Dover was to go to York where the 1st Division would assemble. He sent a telegram to his wife who was living in the New Forest: 'Arrived Dover safely. Go to York'.

In fact the train went to Aberystwyth, but his wife took a train to York. Eventually Hudson contacted her at the Station Hotel. 'She found me fast asleep in an hotel in London, after two ghastly train journeys up and down England on two consecutive nights and endless attempts to get in touch with me. But all that was soon forgotten on our reunion.'

NINE

• • • • • • • •

The Home Front

During the next period of Hudson's life there occurred a series of events which brought out some typical elements of his character: his bloody-minded refusal to submit to authority which he deemed to be misplaced, his determined honesty almost to a fault and his almost heroic refusal to compromise in any moral dilemma, his ability to be dispassionate about his qualities and failings and his acceptance of his fate, however cruel it might be, without enduring bitterness.

His first reaction to life in beleaguered England was astonishment at how much of the population, although sad at the evacuation from Dunkirk, seemed determined to carry on as if nothing much had happened. He and his family were billeted in a large suburban house near Rotherham in Yorkshire. His host was a kindly businessman.

The general opinion seemed to be that we were well rid of unreliable allies, and that now at any rate we knew where we stood. As for invasion, the British Navy would see to that but if some Germans slipped through they would now meet men who were determined to fight. . . . These hard-headed businessmen, kindly as they were in personal relations, could think only in terms of economics and their own depleted pockets or those of their companies.

In social life their wives discussed domestic affairs and their friends and acquaintances' weaknesses, interminably. They entertained endlessly among themselves. Their husbands gathered in corners and still continued to talk business and how to make or save money, including complicated methods of evading income tax. Dunkirk had stirred their generous instincts, but it could not alter their otherwise innate and deep-seated materialism.

There followed an event which, deliberately or not, seems largely to have evaded historians of the period. Hudson was, of course, still commanding his brigade. All officers of his rank or over in the Corps were summoned to a room in a hotel in York for a conference where they would be addressed by a very important person. On arrival they were carefully checked. There they waited speculating as to who the VIP might be, Hudson personally expecting the King.

The door opened and the Chief of the Imperial General Staff, General Dill, appeared ushering in Mr Anthony Eden, the recently appointed Secretary of State for War. Eden, after a few remarks on the gravity of the general situation, wasted little time in coming to the real point of his visit. The Prime Minister, he said, had told the nation in the clearest possible terms his policy for the future. He then quoted from that wonderful broadcast in which Mr Winston Churchill had said that Britain would never give in.

'We shall fight on the beaches, we shall fight on the landing grounds, we shall fight in the fields, we shall fight in the hills; we shall never surrender, and even if, which I do not for a moment believe, this Island or a large part of it were subjugated and starving, then our Empire beyond the seas, armed and guarded by the British Fleet, would carry on the struggle, until, in God's good time, the New World with all its power and might, steps forth to the rescue and liberation of the Old.'

He, Anthony Eden, was responsible to his Chief for seeing that this policy was implemented. His first duty was to find out what the temper of the Army was, so that he could report from personal knowledge to the Prime Minister. He proposed therefore to ask each one of us in turn if, in our opinion, the troops under our command could be counted on to continue the fight in all circumstances.

There was an almost audible gasp all round the table. To us it seemed almost incredible, almost an impertinence, that such a question should be asked of us. Eden, no doubt, and wisely, was not averse to shaking us out of our tendency towards complacency. After a pause he rose again to his feet and said he did not want to appear defeatist in his attitude but we had some very hard facts to face. The Navy could not guarantee to prevent considerable forces from landing on our shores; the Air Force would have to face enormous odds and difficulties. The Army would be for some time pitifully weak in arms and equipment. In spite of everything that might be done, a moment might come when the Government would have to make, at short notice, a terrible decision. That point might come when in the opinion of the Government it would be definitely unwise to throw in, in a futile effort to save a hopeless situation, badly armed men against an enemy firmly lodged in England and in possession of our southern ports, bases and arsenals.

The question he was putting to us, the answer to which would obviously considerably influence the decision to be made at the time, was whether our troops would, if called on, embark at a northern port, say Liverpool, while it was still in our hands, in order to be withdrawn to, say, Canada? Without such a nucleus of trained troops from the Home Country the Prime Minister's declared policy of carrying on the fight from overseas would be infinitely more difficult to carry out.

In dead silence one after the other was asked the question which was now so different in its complexion and implications.

It was not necessary to pose the same question to all the individuals round the table, for it was very soon apparent that all were of much the same opinion. The proportion who would respond to the call among Regular officers would be high. Of Regular NCOs, and men who were unmarried, nearly as high. No one dared, however, to estimate any exact proportion amongst those officers and men who had only come forward for the war; a smaller proportion of unmarried men might respond but the very great majority of these would insist either on fighting it out in England, as they would want to do, or on taking their chances with their families whatever the consequences might be.

Eden then turned to his second point. Was the assembled company in agreement with the proposal that the Army should in fact fight on the beaches and continue, as in the declared policy, to fight every step of the way?

There was almost unanimous agreement with the policy, but, perhaps typically, Hudson 'thought different'. He said that he believed that the best form of defence was attack and that when it became clear that an invasion was imminent a series of small scale raids should be made 'aimed at suitable points along the French and Belgian coasts . . . the enemy would hesitate to launch an invasion fleet of troop-filled barges if at points near the launching areas we had offensive-minded troops on their immediate flank. This method would entail serious risks but to leave the initiative entirely to the enemy was, in his opinion, a greater danger.' There was no support for Hudson's ideas and the conference came to an end.

It was not long after this conference that Hudson was informed that he had been awarded the CB (Companion of the Order of the Bath) for his services during the retreat from Dunkirk. At that time he thought that this was more or less a routine ration dole out for the next on the list. He felt considerable shame, therefore, when Alexander said to him one day: 'You don't seem to appreciate the honour done you in being awarded the CB. Do you realise that only one per corps was allotted for distribution after Dunkirk? You were selected from all the officers of the rank of colonel or over in the first corps, and General Montgomery in the second corps.

'I could only apologise for my seeming ingratitude, for it must obviously have been Alexander who had recommended me.'

All the previous doubts about his suitability for command of a brigade in action, which had been the bane of his life when stationed in Aldershot before the war, were therefore totally dispelled with this honour.

After a conference at the War Office at which Hudson again disagreed with the proposal that all beaches should be defended, it was eventually decided that the role of Hudson's brigade in the event of an invasion should be to be ready to move at the shortest possible notice. Furthermore, that they should carry out a counter-attack at any point on the great arc of the coast of England formed by the counties of Norfolk and Suffolk, a coastline of about a 120 miles. For this purpose they moved to a central point from which the range to the furthest point of the coast was up to 30 or 40 miles, and given civilian charabancs as transport. He discovered to his fury that while the peacetime charabancs were still being used for pleasure trips he was given old and decrepit vehicles which often broke down. This only confirmed his conviction that the British people and some of its leaders simply did not appreciate the mortal danger in which they lay.

During the next few weeks there were other signs of the same phenomenon. When Hudson had insisted on his brigade practising their action in the event of an invasion in his area twice a week, there were grumbles both from the battalions under him and from higher authority. When he had signs fixed to the telegraph poles showing the various routes to the coast he was told that this was against Post Office regulations. He was inclined to ask if a German invasion was also against Post Office regulations. When his Brigade was sent to Inveraray in Scotland to train in landing operations he was appalled to find that little had been done about the construction of landing craft. There were insufficient numbers even for training purposes with one brigade. In fact, the lack of landing craft would have put paid to the ideas he had advanced about constant raids on the French and Belgian coasts to disrupt German invasion plans.

When Hudson was at Inveraray he stayed with the Duke of Argyll.

He was a charming old man and host, but he was a full-blooded autocrat, and just could not understand modern democratic ideas. As a staunch loyalist he was prepared to accept sacrifice up to his own standard of limit. But that soldiers should be allowed to roam at will over his moors, and erect tents and even huts in his private park, was beyond that limit. What, he asked, would happen to the deer?'

It had not entered my mind to wonder if, and when, I was going to be promoted Major-General until I got hints from one of the staff. From these I gathered there were doubts in some people's minds as to my fitness to command a Division. I had my own doubts, for there is a great difference between a Brigade and a Division. However that was other people's responsibility and I was not in the least worried. Then, at very short notice I was told by phone I had been promoted to command a Division then serving on the Scottish border between Edinburgh and Glasgow. I was to report to my new headquarters within forty-eight hours.

On his arrival he was immediately plunged into a most unfortunate drama. His Chief Administrative Staff Officer came to see him to say that one of the commanding officers of a battalion in his division was challenging the authority of his brigade commander. The colonel, a large colliery owner, had raised from his own colliery the battalion he was commanding. He acted as if the battalion was his own private army. The culminating clash with his brigadier came when, shortly after an order had been promulgated that officers were not to use their official cars on private journeys, the brigadier had found out that the colonel, without asking for permission to leave his station, had used his official car to go to Nottingham. Hudson immediately said that the Brigadier was to put the colonel under open arrest (an action which entailed the culprit being suspended from his duty and kept under surveillance until a court of enquiry or a court martial could be set up). The Staff Officer, somewhat taken aback, said that there were some complications. The colonel was a Member of Parliament, he had been summoned urgently to dine in Nottingham with Winston Churchill and had not had time to ask for permission to leave his station. Furthermore, the Speaker of the House of Commons must immediately be told that one of his MPs had been arrested and given the reasons for the action.

Hudson replied that he had no intention of starting his new job by not supporting one of his brigadiers and ordered the arrest to go ahead.

Next day Hudson received a plethora of telephone calls and telegrams from the War Office and the Commander in Chief Scottish Command and others. He was told that the dinner was not a private one but a public function at which the colonel had been asked to propose Winston Churchill's health. Hudson still refused to change his mind and even offered to resign his command if that would help. The situation was eventually resolved by transferring the battalion which, unfortunately, came from Hudson's own original regiment, the Sherwood Foresters, to another division where the commander was more amenable and the arrest was cancelled.

The affair ended with the colonel, in a great gesture of magnanimity, asking Hudson to inspect his battalion before it was transferred and making a fulsome speech in Hudson's honour as an old officer of the regiment. 'In private he apologised for the whole unfortunate affair and we parted with mutual expressions of good will.'

It is difficult, if not impossible, to make judgements about incidents of this kind. There are clear arguments on both sides, but it does appear on the surface that Hudson had made a mistake in sticking to his order when the full circumstances had been revealed, but his character was such that, even in retrospect, his actions were probably inevitable.

Hudson's division was then transferred to Norfolk to act as a reserve to the divisions on the coast in the event of an invasion. Hudson was told by a friend – a general on the Home Forces staff – that his new corps commander had a reputation for sacking his subordinates, but that he should not worry too much, as he was unlikely to last long.

My interview with my new Corps Commander was not at first encouraging, though it ended on a happier note. I could not quite make out whether he was deliberately rude because he wanted to see my reaction or because he was deficient in both manners and imagination. He referred to my being the holder of a VC and made the sort of remarks which I had heard occasionally before from people who are obviously professionally jealous. He said he had had a Brigadier VC under him in France, and he had been a splendid chap but one of the stupidest men he had ever known. He had, he said, never known a VC who was not charming nor one who was capable of commanding more than a battalion in peacetime, or a Brigade in war. He hoped he had now met the exception to the rule!

The corps commander had been in the Royal Corps of Signals and Hudson found him rather a pathetic figure who chain-smoked continually to calm his shaken nerves. 'He lived in continual fear of being passed over for promotion.' There were only two divisions in the corps, one on the coast and of little tactical interest for it was fully extended along the beaches. The corps commander began to occupy himself solely with Hudson's division, visiting it without telling Hudson that he was doing so and generally grossly interfering in Hudson's handling of his command.

> He visited battalions and wrote copious notes about their training and administration direct to battalion or Brigade Commanders. He ran exercises for officers or attended mine and in these he generally seemed to manage to place himself in opposition to myself in any argument that arose. He even asked me to assemble my officers so that an outside lecturer on training could address them at my Headquarters, under his chairmanship. The culminating point came when, acting as Corps Commander in his absence, I found a letter in my basket from a battalion Commander in my own Division which referred to an operation called 'Stag' of which I had never heard. The opening sentence of a second letter, also from a battalion Commander read: 'You asked me to let you know direct . . . .' I had been strictly loyal to my Corps Commander in the fullest meaning of the word but I felt that a limit must be set to this private correspondence with my subordinates behind my back which was in time bound to undermine my authority and lead possibly to unpleasant complications.

Hudson then wrote an official letter of complaint, mentioning the two letters he had found and quoting other incidents of a similar nature. He received no answer for a time and then he was visited by the corps commander who was very conciliatory and promised not to interfere with his division. 'He was ultra-friendly and almost sentimental.' Hudson agreed to tear his letter up and not to refer to it again. The corps commander said he was going on a fortnight's leave and on his return he would 'mend his ways'.

On his return, however, the corps commander came to see Hudson and told him that he had just realised that Hudson's rank as a major-general would be confirmed shortly – six months after he had taken up the job – and that it would then be much more difficult to get rid of him. He handed Hudson an official report in which he stated that he was, in his opinion, unfit to command a division. He ended the conversation, surprisingly, by saying that he hoped Hudson would not think he was taking the course he had in order to save his skin. He went on to say that Hudson was free to appeal against the decision. He did so.

Meanwhile I had been trying to look at the whole matter as objectively as I could. The important point was whether or not I was fitted to command a Division: nothing else really mattered. On this point I was by no means confident. The Corps Commander had said that there was a great gulf fixed between a first-class Brigade Commander, as he conceded I might have been, and a reasonably good Divisional Commander. I knew this was true. I felt that I did not really fit the bill as a General in some important respects. I was not 'showman' enough. Round a conference table or during large-scale training exercise, when I was asked to express an opinion without previous preparation, I was apt to make a poor showing. On the other hand, though I might be too reckless, I felt that on active services I had qualities which perhaps justified my retention, though this was a point which I could hardly make in cold blood in any protest.

Alexander who knew me as a Commander in war was in the Middle East, or I might have asked for his advice and championship.

The War Office representative who came to see me had told me in so many words that the Corps Commander's report was regarded with grave suspicion. In the course of conversation I told him 'off the record' of the letter I had written to the Corps Commander and the reason I had done so. I told him too that I had agreed to regard this episode as closed, and that I was not prepared to mention it in any protest I now made without further consideration. He left me in no doubt that should I mention the letter it would have a very considerable bearing on the ultimate decision on my case.

In the event, Hudson was summoned to the War Office. The general who interviewed him was clearly aware of the letter Hudson had written (he had told his senior staff officer who must have passed it on) and tried to get him to refer to it as a reason for his sacking. Hudson had been told that if he allowed the letter to be used in evidence against the corps commander his case would be looked at again but he had given his word not to mention it again and he refused to do so.

Hudson handed over his division to an old and sympathetic friend and went on leave. He had to take down the general's insignia on his uniform and revert to his substantive rank of Colonel. 'There are few blows in life which are more shattering than wounded pride. I felt personally shamed and disgraced. I had worn the insignia of a general long enough to become known to relatives, friends and acquaintances as such, and now I had to tell them that I had dropped to a rank lower than that I had held before the war.'

He tried to look at the whole affair as objectively as he could. He knew that he did not really fit the bill in some respects. The die, however, was cast and he faced the future hoping for an active command of some kind.

He did get command of a brigade, in Northern Ireland – not a very active theatre. During his stay there, apart from routine training, there were two incidents of note. In conditions of the utmost secrecy, dressed in civilian clothes, he was sent to the South in order to reconnoitre routes for a possible, although extremely unlikely, invasion of the South. The U-boat campaign against British merchant shipping was becoming extremely efficient and Britain was in some danger of being starved out. The British Navy was hampered by not being able to use the Irish ports which meant that escort vessels had to travel many miles further on the way to the scene of action than would have been the case if the Irish ports were available to them. It had been decided, as a very last resort, that if the moment came when real starvation threatened the nation, it might be necessary to consider whether or not to secure these ports for Britain for British Naval use by an invasion. There were very large numbers of Southern Irish serving in the British forces (in fact a higher proportion of the population than that of Northern Ireland itself which never had conscription) and it is impossible to know what their reaction would have been to the invasion by Britain of their home country. The situation, however, never even approached starvation levels and the question of invasion never arose.

The second event was the arrival of some American forces in Northern Ireland. One battalion – the first to come to Europe – came under Hudson's command for a river-crossing exercise. The American battalion was in reserve in order to counter-attack if the enemy crossed the river.

The Americans had been training in the great open spaces of the southern states of America with broad roads on which to move. They had immense motor carriers, which could hardly move at all down the narrow Northern Ireland lanes, and only with the greatest difficulty did they reach their allotted area at all.

When I went to see them I found them enthusiastically keen. I explained that I would call on them to make one of three possible counter-attacks to regain control of a blown bridge site. I was assured I had only to give the word and could leave the rest to them. In due course the 'enemy' made their assault-boat crossing at about 2 a.m. I at once sent off my young American liaison officer on his powerful motorbike with orders to return with the expected hour of his battalion's advance.

After a long wait I sent one of our officers and he returned to tell me that the whole battalion had firmly retired to rest in their camp beds, wearing pyjamas. The Commanding Officer, roused with difficulty, had said that after they had waited all day for the order to counter-attack he had supposed they would not be called on that night and the battalion must now be given time to get their breakfasts. I realised for the first time how unrealistic was the American conception of war at that time.

Hudson then received an order to go on embarkation leave immediately as he was shortly to go to Cyprus as a major-general to take command of the garrison, which was to be brought up to the strength of a division. He was to be flown out from an airfield near Burley, in the New Forest, where his wife and son were living at the time. He had his major-general's insignia sewn on his uniform again and was walking across the tarmac towards the aeroplane when he was given a telegram cancelling his appointment. He was to return to his brigade in Northern Ireland.

The Commander-in-Chief in Northern Ireland was an old friend, General Franklin. One day he told Hudson that the Chief of the Imperial General Staff, General Brooke, wanted to see him. Brooke said that General Alexander, commanding in the Middle East was glad when Hudson was to be sent to Cyprus under his command but the scare had died down and it had been decided not to form a division there. He added, however, that Hudson need not worry as he would be given a division at the first available opportunity.

Shortly afterwards the division was sent to England and when Hudson's brigade was stationed near St Albans he received a telegram from his wife to say that his son, John, had been killed in action in North Africa. This was a shattering blow. He and his wife later learnt that John had been leading his platoon in an attack when a machine gun had opened up on them. John 'had jumped up and had tried to lead them forward but the machine gun opened up again and he fell. He was later carried back to the regimental aid post where he died.' Hudson had never really recovered from the anguish of leaving his son behind on his posting to Singapore many years before. He was consumed by remorse and grief.

The brigade was then moved to Dover which was just in shell range of the Germans in France, but they did not open fire unless the British fired first. He had not been there long when General Franklin called to see him. He said that the selection

committee which appointed senior officers had turned Hudson
down to command a division on account of his age – he was
just over the recently imposed age limit of 48. This, Franklin
said, would have been waived if it had not been for one nigger
in the woodpile. Hudson never discovered who he was. As he
put it in his journal:

> Being in principle, and I hope in practice, against the colour bar
> I am quite prepared to accept that a nigger, even in a woodpile,
> can be right.
>
> Franklin then told me that it was obvious that age would now
> bar my employment in an active command. He had studied the
> vacancies in various types of employment available and had
> found one which he thought I would prefer to a routine
> administrative command. It involved my going to Iraq to
> command the local Levies. He would recommend me for the job,
> if I wished, and anticipated no difficulty over this. It was the best
> he could do, and he advised me to go unless I had any particular
> objection to a hot climate. I accepted his advice.

TEN
· · · · · · · ·

The Middle East

On New Year's Day 1944 Hudson found himself on a Dutch ship bound for Port Said. He was seconded to the RAF as they were responsible for the Iraqi Levies. The ship was full of RAF officers and men. They were entirely concerned with base maintenance. There were no pilots aboard. Hudson found a very different atmosphere from that of the Army he had been used to. The men had been recruited during the war mainly from factories where there was an 'us' and 'them' relationship with their owners. The officers called their men 'erks' and the men had not much regard for their officers.

He was given a lift by an ATS (the female element of the British Army) colonel from Port Said to Cairo, which he had always disliked, very conscious of the atmosphere of disdain and insolence between the Arabs and their British overlords. He eventually found his way to Habbaniya about 30 miles from Baghdad where the RAF had an air station and where the Iraqi Levies were based. There were two other air stations, one, Shaiba, near Basra in the south, the other at Mosul in the north. At Basra there was a large number of ugly sprawling dumps of stores to be guarded.

The Iraqi Levies originated after the First World War, when the Assyrians, a Christian people who lived in the mountains north of Mesopotamia (Iraq), were driven by the Turks out of their mountain homes. [*Author's note* – there is much controversy about the origins of the Assyrian people. It is certain that they suffered great persecution by the Turks in the late 19th and early 20th centuries in the same period as the Armenian massacres and that some 700,000 Assyrian Christians lost their lives. It has been said that the Assyrians were originally converted to Christianity by St Thomas.] They had thrown in their lot with the British, who had promised them protection and ultimate resettlement. Protection for their families was provided within the wired perimeter of Habbaniya and the men were formed into a military force.

All attempts at a resettlement after the war failed. About 20,000 Assyrians remained in Habbaniya. Some returned to small settlements in Kurdistan, many emigrated to America and others settled in Persia (Iran). The Levies were in great demand in the Second World War but mainly as guards for RAF aerodromes, though they had been in action against the Iraqi army earlier in the war. Recruits came down from the mountains and from a small settlement on the Khabour River in Syria. The RAF pressed for more and more Levies to guard air stations in the Persian Gulf States, Persia, Palestine, Cyprus and the Lebanon. This had been met by recruiting Kurds from the mountains, Arabs from the southern deserts of Iraq, Baluchis from Northern India and one or two companies of a strange tribe of hill men from northern Iraq called Yazidis. These latter were Satan worshippers, the Assyrians were Christian, the rest were Muslim and the mixture did not always make for peaceful relationships.

This extraordinary force was under the command of the RAF, but it was officered entirely by seconded British Army officers and a portion of British Army NCOs. There were also eighteen

RAMC doctors most of whom, under a British RAF Senior Medical Officer, were Jewish refugees.

To control this remarkable command, spread over the whole of the Middle East except Africa, Hudson had a brigade major and two administrative staff officers and, later, one intelligence officer. He had under him also five British battalion commanders, two in Habbaniya, one in northern Iraq and Persia, one in Basra and the Persian Gulf, another in Palestine and a senior major in Cyprus. He also added a sixth battalion commander for North Palestine and the Lebanon.

The job he had was an enormous contrast to anything he had previously encountered, but he threw himself into it with great gusto. He had no difficulty in getting RAF aeroplanes to take him around the area in which his command lay and he spent a lot of his time trying to get in touch with the village communities in the mountainous region north of Iraq from where he drew his men and to which they returned on leave.

During the spring months the annual war broke out between the Iraqi Army and the local tribesmen. During these outbreaks British officers were warned off. In the winter months snow prevented movement in the higher altitudes so Hudson had to be careful how he picked his time for tours. He generally went with a henchman, an Assyrian, who was welcome in both Kurdish and Assyrian villages. Everyone carried arms but shots were fired only if a villager strayed out of his village grazing area, unless some particular blood feud had started up. The Iraqi government had some police posts along the few roads, but the police very rarely left them. On one of his five-day tours Hudson wrote to his wife:

They are Chaldeans in this part of the country. The Chaldean priests are properly trained in a Roman Catholic college in Mosul for twelve years and the best become bishops and go to Rome for five years. The Nestorians just pick a man in the village as a deacon though the best have been to a missionary school. The

Nestorian bishops, of whom I have met three, are simple old men, whereas the Chaldean bishops seem grasping and cunning. Nevertheless, I met one old Chaldean village priest who had retired. He was 85. He was the perfect happy old man, surrounded by his tribesmen who all regarded him as a prophet and leader. He said he had a son, an interpreter to the English at Kirkuk, another to the French at Beirut and added, 'And I, I am the interpreter of God', at which he, and all with him, laughed delightedly. His daughter was in America. I asked him if he heard from her. He held out his hand, steady as a rock, but said 'Now when I try to write my hand seems to shake and my writing is like the tracks of a bird hopping here and there in the snow.

The villages consisted of mud houses built into the sides of the hills, flat-roofed, and we sat and slept in them. On arrival we were given drinks (arak) and little bits of meat, then masses of grapes, then dinner or lunch at any hour, rice and more meat and tough chicken, and endless smoking. It is all very peaceful but the stories are all the time of feuds, the stealing of sheep and murders – a curious mixture.

All loathe the Iraqis and the Kurds are organising for a fight. British can go anywhere and all the tribesmen are, or have been, Levies. I am regarded as a great man, all powerful, and I keep on explaining that I am a soldier and not a political officer.

The Assyrian women, who remain in the background, wear handkerchiefs of gay and variegated colours over their heads, high-necked blouses and very full and long skirts. Assyrians are very Victorian in their sex morals. The Kurds keep their women out of sight, though they have a peep if they can. In both cases I gathered that there were a good many strong-minded women who rule the lazy men. Mothers are held in more esteem than wives.

The Assyrian Christian priests informed Hudson of the conditions in the villages and the thoughts and needs of the Assyrian soldiers. The Kurdish mullahs on the other hand were far less forthcoming. They were suspicious of the intentions of the British whom they regarded as backing the Iraqis against them.

There was serious poverty among both races. Clothing shortage was a great problem. The art and means of weaving had practically died out and there was a great shortage of sheep's wool. Cheap clothing from Mosul and Baghdad had killed local weaving in peacetime. Hudson immediately set about trying to revive weaving in the villages. He obtained the design of a suitable loom and had several made by the RAF.

> I was lucky to find one of our British NCOs had been a foreman in a Bradford factory and he soon learned from the Jews how to handle the wooden hand looms. Carefully selecting from thirty volunteer Levies who came from well-separated villages, I handed them over to the Sergeant to try out. From these he chose twenty-four who were teachable. These ran our twelve looms for long hours.

By the time Hudson left, the project was flourishing.

In the force itself, Kurds and Assyrians were kept in separate companies and there was no trouble. The Assyrians were hard-pressed in their villages and only the lure of pay kept the men from going home or brought them back from their four-monthly leave periods. To go on leave they went by train to Mosul and by the normal bus service up the road into the hills and then walked. The village Hudson's Assyrian servant came from was a three-day walk from the end of the road. 'By custom, the bus itself was neutral ground, and bitter enemies might sit or stand side-by-side on the bus but, after dismounting, the traveller had to watch his step and choose his route with circumspection.' Hudson describes the travails of the Assyrians:

> Generally speaking, what can be said of most 'displaced persons' can be said of the Assyrians. In their case a whole nation was displaced. The League of Nations undertook to resettle them as a

nation but all attempts failed. This was partly because no country would receive them and partly because they really only wished to return to their historic homelands, by then overrun and occupied by fighting Muslim tribes over whom no one had any authority. The Assyrians are a nation, but they were also tribesmen, and tribal jealousies invariably broke out when any combined attempt or concerted effort was required. This had consistently been their undoing. . . . A number of schemes for settlement had been tried. Canada nearly took them, Australia refused them over the colour bar though, apart from sunburn, they were nearer white than black. A scheme to move them to an area in the north-east of Africa fell through. Curiously, money was not the difficulty. The Foreign Office was prepared to put up a very substantial sum, and the League of Nations would have helped.

A further scheme of settlement on the Khabour River on the boundary between Iraq and Syria was tried, which could have been a success if the Assyrians had pulled together, but soon after it was begun quarrelling intervened and it was never continued. Typically, and undaunted by the difficulties, Hudson put forward a scheme of his own. Near Habbaniya was a large lake. Beyond it was a large depression where no one lived. There were many examples, notably in Palestine, where irrigation had 'made the desert flower' and Hudson drew up an outline scheme for an Assyrian settlement in this depression. He took it to the British Ambassador who passed it on to the Foreign Office. After months had gone by Hudson was told that in view of the imminence of a renewal of the British Iraqi Treaty 'the question would not be raised at present with the Iraqi Government.' [*Author's note*: this depression was later, in the 1950s, to be used as an area into which the flood waters of the Tigris would be diverted, thus preventing flooding round Baghdad and greatly improving conditions there.]

Hudson was in Syria when Paris fell to the Allies in 1944 and went to a party to celebrate. The French mayor and general made stirring speeches on the prowess of the magnificent French Army who had liberated Paris. The British and American armies were only once referred to as allies and General de Gaulle not at all. 'This was, I suppose, hardly surprising, as the French present had all been supporters of the Vichy regime,' said Hudson.

The Iraqi Levies had a number of detachments in Persia and Hudson had an absorbing time visiting them all, bouncing over barely made up tracks to villages in the far north as well as more formal visits to Kermanshah, Hamadan and, above all, to Teheran. He found conditions in Persia 'horrifying'.

Peasants were half-starved because the over-wealthy merchants and landowners seized the fruit of their labours. In the towns, beggars fell dead of disease and want in the streets. The contrast between the poverty of the workers and the wealth of the employers was appalling. I could only with difficulty eat a dinner at an extravagant price in the brightly illuminated garden of a first-class hotel, while above, on the public road, rows of half-starved onlookers, mostly children, peered hungrily over a low wall.

There are still areas in Northern Persia which travellers have hardly ever visited and while carrying out some training at our camp at Karina, we took a jeep and went on a visit of exploration to some very remote villages. The driver was the Commander of a RAF armoured car company. I sat next to him, and our doctor and a Persian speaking Levy officer made up the party. At the far end of a gradually deteriorating cart trail we came on a village. The villagers turned out in force to receive us; their main object, apart from normal curiosity, was to beg us to cure an important member of their small community. He was a burly man, and he had an arm in such a dreadful condition that I could not bear to look at it. Our doctor, having no such qualms, examined it carefully and gave him some sort of injection, but told us that only amputation could save his life. We could not possibly take him back to civilisation in our already overcrowded jeep, but I felt very guilty at leaving this wretched man to his fate.

A small stream barred our further progress, but the villagers, with very little encouragement, felled trees and within a few hours we had crossed. The track had become only a mule track, winding through the mountains, but a jeep is powerful enough and yet light enough to be taken almost anywhere by four men prepared to force a way through.

The village we eventually reached was in a wooded dell through which a stream flowed, a most attractive retreat. The villagers had frequently seen aeroplanes flying overhead but they had never seen a motorcar. They refused to believe we had come across country and could not believe we had not got wings somewhere tucked away in the jeep which we could unfold. We had a wireless reception set and that evening managed to give them a concert. They could not understand why we could not repeat a tune they happened to like.

The highlight of the evening was when their own particular village headman was addressed down the wireless in person. This feat was accomplished by the Levy officer slipping away unseen and speaking in Persian down a remote control instrument which we had with us. The headman shouted his answering speech down the wireless set amidst great applause.

From Teheran Hudson drove south, another 200 miles, to Isfahan. Part of the road was used by American and British convoys carrying stores to the Russians.

Suddenly after miles of utter desolation, broken only by stony ravines, we came round a corner onto one of the most astonishingly beautiful views I have ever seen. The beauty of Isfahan from a distance is no doubt greatly enhanced by its desolate approach. The city stands spread out below the approach road, in a fertile plain in the bowl of the hills, watered by the

Zayendeh, a broad river crossed by three fine bridges. The banks of the river are lined with avenues, gardens and orchards, which intermingle with the buildings, mosques, palaces and Minarets.

Hudson's next venture was to initiate and run a major Tattoo in Baghdad. The main feature of the daylight air display was to be a drop by the Levies' newly formed parachute company. Initially, little enthusiasm was shown by the RAF, but, after some hesitation, the British Ambassador in Baghdad agreed and a visit to Cairo secured the enthusiastic support of the air officer commanding, Air Chief Marshal Sir Keith Park. Powerful Army searchlights were sent all the way by road from Egypt. The RAF Central Middle East Band was promised together with teams of gymnasts and motorcyclists. Money was provided. Kurdish and Assyrian dancers and tightrope walkers from the hills proved wonderfully popular. The drill item by the Levies and the torchlight procession and its intricacies led up to the sudden and unexpected formation of the letters RAF.

We had arranged two full dress performances at Habbaniya at which hundreds of desert Arabs provided an overwhelmingly enthusiastic and astonished audience. Extra performances had to be laid on and we only just managed to transfer the show to Baghdad in time for the opening performance which was a tremendous success.

Hudson sat next to the boy King Faisal of Iraq.

He was wildly excited and all attempts to restrain him by his stern Scottish nanny failed. Our parachute British Sergeant-Instructor cleverly managed to drop within a few yards of his front row seat to present him with a large box of chocolates, suitably got up in RAF colours. The dignitaries present, the Regent, the Ambassador, the Air Officer Commander-in-Chief and the rest, were nearly enveloped in his parachute.

Seeing a number of vultures flying high above the aeroplanes as they came in for the drop, the young King remarked, 'I wonder what they think of birds that fly without any wings?' To Lady Park he said, 'I suppose you have travelled to many countries. You ought to get something in each country. I will bring you something from mine tomorrow.' Next day, on which he insisted on seeing the Tattoo again, he produced a copper 10 *fils* piece (a farthing) very secretively out of his pocket and whispered to me did I think, he asked, 'the English lady whom I sat next to the day before would like it?' I assured him that she would treasure it all her life, and I hope she has.

Following the Tattoo, I got a handsome letter of thanks from the Ambassador. I tried not to think of the relative futility of my struggles to put on a tattoo, in wartime, when life and death battles were being organised and fought elsewhere.

During this period Hudson was told that he had been made an ADC to the King of Britain! This greatly impressed the Iraqi Levies, but in fact he never had to carry out any duties as ADC.

There were many opportunities for sport of all kinds in Habbaniya and Hudson joined in with gusto, playing polo, squash, tennis, hunting jackal, riding horses in races, shooting duck and francolin and water skiing. He also went skiing in the mountains behind Beirut. The whole Iraqi episode was an amazing contrast to the life and death struggles in Europe, but there was nothing Hudson could do about that and he made the most of his opportunities.

He visited Palestine and as a Christian was overwhelmed by the thought that Jesus Christ himself 'had walked these hills' and struggled up the Via Dolorosa. He also went to Cyprus where he had a company of Kurds. He had detachments of Baluchis (from India) in Sharja, Kuwait and Bahrain.

Not surprisingly, with such a mixed force, there were a number of racial and cultural problems which Hudson had to attempt to sort out with some, but not total, success. On one occasion Hudson's Arab companies were all in the Basra area and one day he was told that a powerful Arab Sheikh had sent his son to ask for the return of one of his slaves who had run away and joined the Levies. The Sheikh had offered the adjutant £500 to get the man back. Hudson told the colonel that he must mollify the Sheikh as best he could, but he would never be a party to handing a slave over to the terrible fate that awaited him when he returned.

Later the true facts came out – the slave himself was anxious to return. He was in fact an illegitimate son born of a slave mother. He had been brought up in his master's household and had become the boon companion of the Sheikh's own son and heir. The two young men had had a serious quarrel and the slave had run away. He now wished to return. Hudson authorised his release.

On another occasion Hudson gave a dinner for a visiting Sheikh of great importance in his area. After dinner they sat in the garden while a film was shown. Hudson did not realise that the Sheikh had never seen a film before and when a gangster advanced firing a revolver the Sheikh drew his own weapon and fired back. The film show had to come to an end.

My predecessor had only agreed to send companies as far as Palestine on the understanding that the men would still be given the same leave as they had had in Iraq. One day while I was in Habbaniya, I heard that the RAF Headquarters in Cairo had asked Palestine Headquarters to supply guards for aerodromes in Italy. Regarding my companies as operationally under them, the Palestine Headquarters had ordered two companies of Assyrians to prepare to go there. The men, fearing the promise made to them would be broken, had flatly refused to carry out any duty as a protest against the order and their officers were powerless. That morning wire and telephone messages poured in upon me – my Levies were in a state of mutiny, what was I going to do about it? They must be disarmed at once, a British battalion in

Palestine had been ordered to stand by, etc. etc. There was an outstanding 'flap' on, as the expressive phrase goes.

I got into an aeroplane and flew direct to Cairo, for it was obvious I could do little without such authority as I could get from the overlord of both Palestine and Iraq. The Air Officer Commanding in the Middle East at the time was Sholto Douglas, Marshal of the Royal Air Force. On reaching Cairo I was led to his room in an atmosphere of hushed awe and ushered in, rather as if I were being admitted into a lion's cage, with very little expectation of ever coming out alive. In fact, as in the case of most big men, he could not have been more sympathetic. After listening calmly to my story, he told a staff officer to phone Palestine that they were to cancel the order the men objected to if I were to require it of them. I offered to try to get volunteers for Italy if I could and by late afternoon I was in the camp of the first of the two protesting companies.

My address to both companies was much the same and the result was identical. I failed to get any volunteers. The first company was inclined to be rebellious and there were at first some rather ugly moments but I was able to prevent what I had feared, that some excitable soldiers would take some action that could not be overlooked. One or two courts martial of ringleaders did in the end result but the sentences were comparatively light and the offenders were hotheads who were well got rid of for a time in any case. The order was withdrawn and all went well.

One of the more bizarre features of Hudson's stay in Iraq concerned the recruits the Levies had from the Yazidis (*see* page 192): 'Very few of them had any knowledge whatever of the world outside their own restricted territory, and fewer Europeans had any knowledge of them, beyond the fact that they were devil worshippers.' They prided themselves on being a 'people of a Book', but no outsider had ever seen their Book, which was only available to their chieftain. They believed in Satan (whose name must never be mentioned). When as a defaulting archangel he was turned out of heaven, they alone of all peoples of the earth continued to stand by him. When, therefore, in the course of time he is received back they will be raised to great power and glory. Many curious customs have grown into their lives. One of these is that they must never have anything to do with the colour green. This they say arose because when Satan fell to earth he landed in a cabbage patch. The shock of finding himself among the green cabbages was so great that he declared their colour to be abhorrent.

The head of the Yazidis was a young boy of about 12. His two uncles acted as regents. Hearing that all three would be prepared to accept an invitation to Habbaniya to see their tribesmen, I arranged a visit. The boy chief was a very good looking young man of a type far superior to any of his tribesmen – the regents were unusually tall, bearded and fierce looking. I had been told that the boy chief desired above all else a camera about which he had been told by his uncles. A programme was laid on where certain members would be formally introduced. Then his party would be led into the garden, a photo would be taken and the camera presented. As we left for the meeting my Chief Levy Officer rushed towards me and whispered something I did not catch. But as I entered the garden I saw a battery of chairs arranged for the photos and to my horror the leather of the two principle armchairs in the centre was bright green. There could have been no more deadly insult, and I had to hustle the regents and their chief away before they saw the offending chairs, while they were changed.

Hudson had another strange and rather alarming encounter with local customs. He was asked to a race meeting given by an Arab sheikh.

At an enormous meal before the meeting the Sheikh said he had arranged for me to be given the best horse in his herds. I was somewhat taken aback, but could hardly refuse to ride, although

I was not dressed for the part. The meeting was not at all of the kind I had expected. Two long rows of horsemen were lined up a considerable distance apart facing each other. Most horsemen were carrying rifles. The Sheikh, as starter, mounted in the centre, fired a shot and galloped clear of the course. There followed a head-on charge. Added to the excitement of the yells of riders and spectators, the thundering of the horses hooves, was the apparently inevitable clash, every rider who owned a rifle firing it into the air just before we met. My stallion was in any case by then well out of control, but I had sufficient sense to make no effort to direct him and he passed me through unscathed. Few accidents actually occurred, but there were one or two head-on collisions, much to the delight of the crowd. No side seemed to be declared the winner. No betting took place, it was pure sport!

The Levies were used almost exclusively in the rather boring job of protecting airfields and stores, but the parachute company of Assyrians and Kurds expected and hoped to take part in active combat. In the event they were sent to Italy on the Adriatic coast. Eventually they were told to cross the Adriatic and to capture a battery of German guns perched on a hilltop overlooking a small port in Yugoslavia. They had not been trained to land on a coast from landing craft; however they did so at night. Once ashore, the steep climb meant nothing to these hill men – they reached their objective and captured the battery intact.

It proved to be a German battery sent down from the Russian front for a rest! One platoon captured a number of Germans in a small building near the battery site. The British officer was short of men and had to push on, so he told the Germans to face the wall and left two Kurds with Sten guns to look after them. Just as he was leaving the building a Kurd said, 'Do we have to shoot them all, Sir?'

Later the company was sent to Athens to take part in street fighting, another role for which they were entirely unprepared.

When the war finally ended, Hudson was asked to stay on in command of the Levies 'but my family in England had too great an attraction for me ever to consider such an idea'. In some ways the job of commanding the Iraqi Levies was ideal for Hudson. He was left on his own and had no jealous or prying boss interfering with his projects. He had a fascinating command with great opportunities for examining the very varied area of which he had no previous experience and every opportunity for innovation in every sense of that word. He had enjoyed himself. His return to an exhausted England must have been rather an anti-climax.

ELEVEN

• • • • • • • • • • • • •

Germany

When Hudson's distant cousin Lord Mackenzie died he left Hudson a considerable sum of money and his house in Edinburgh, as did Lord Mackenzie's brother. For the first time in his life Hudson found himself well off, if not rich. His wife bought a house in Devon and he returned home, at first devoting his considerable energies to cutting down trees and generally tidying the small wood on a hill behind the house and planting an acre or so of Christmas trees he intended to sell later.

Out of the blue there appeared a letter from the War Office, asking if Hudson would like to join the British Control Commission in Germany. Feeling he still had something to offer, Hudson agreed to do the job for a year and, having attended a course in England on the organisation and objects of the British Mission, which controlled the Civil Administration of the British Sector in Germany, he left for the Ruhr Valley in November 1946.

The school in England, the journey and my first arrival in Germany were eye-openers of the trend of feeling in post-war Britain. I was plunged into an atmosphere of revolt against war and all its horrors and a determination to forget it. In doing so, its values, including its ideals of brotherhood in the face of danger, were being ruthlessly scrubbed.

I soon found there was a deep and bitter feeling in the Control Commission between the ex-civilian and the ex-soldier. This was still further exacerbated by the political rift between Labour and Conservative, Socialist and Capitalist. Class hatred was alarmingly strong. At first it never occurred to me that the fact that I used the designation of my rank, Brigadier, would cause so strong a prejudice against me from the great majority of those with whom I was to have dealings. Again and again at the school and on the journey, when I gave my name as Brigadier, the clerk or Commission officer would repeat emphatically and pointedly 'Mr Hudson'. I noted too that any chance that presented itself of 'putting me in my place', by giving me the poorest accommodation, or keeping me waiting, and so on, was taken. I comforted myself with an amused realisation that a little humbling would certainly do me no harm.

A further possible difficulty lay in the fact that, not surprisingly, many of the ex-soldiers who were his superiors in Germany had served under him in the Army. This latter situation, however, caused no problems and indeed the ex-soldiers fell over backwards to help in every possible way they could, including arranging decent accommodation and other necessities of life in the general chaos existing at the time in Germany.

Hudson found a vast difference between the executive branch on the one hand, who were most upright and respectable people doing their best to exercise their function of government through the existing German civil administration, and the British Control Officers whose duties entailed the control of German industry on the other. These latter people were of very doubtful quality. It was most unlikely that a trained engineer or mining expert would take on a job in the Commission which gave him no security of tenure or future prospect. As a result only the failures or potential failures joined the Commission, or the very young who were attracted by the high initial pay. Most unfortunately, many of these people became corrupted by the large rewards which the German firms over whom they had considerable power were able to offer.

After some further training Hudson was sent as Kreis Resident Officer to Iserlohn in the Ruhr, where the British Army Corps Headquarters was situated. In theory he was in charge of the whole administration of his area, the equivalent in Britain of a district or borough council. In practice he had to work with and through the existing Burgomeister, the official who, under the German system, had almost complete powers – vastly more than his equivalent in Britain. The particular Burgomeister with whom Hudson had to deal had been incarcerated in German concentration camps for six years owing to his anti-Hitler views. He had a strong character and political ambitions and owned some local German newspapers. He resented the British occupation of his country and his main objective was to regain national freedom. He took every chance to show up any mistake or weakness in the action or activities of the Control Commission, which he did mainly by publishing allegedly private letters to his newspapers and occasionally by editorials. When questioned on these activities he pointed out that one of the main freedoms which the British were trying to inculcate into his country was the freedom of the press. He also, occasionally, made bitterly anti-British speeches.

Although they came to respect each other's point of view their relationship was never easy. The town of Iserlohn had been largely destroyed by aerial bombardment. There were large numbers of refugees flooding the area and one of Hudson's main tasks was, in conjunction with the Burgomeister, the allocation of housing. During the final phases of the war the Ruhr had been very heavily bombed, during the night by the RAF and by day by the Americans. Practically speaking, only the cellars of houses remained, with here and there a 'bunker' above ground intact. A bunker was an air-raid shelter constructed like the inside of a honeycomb. Any houses that had been reconstructed, mostly on the outskirts of the towns or near barracks which the Allies had carefully avoided bombing so their troops could use them, were at once taken over by the occupation troops. The Germans lived in the cellars, which were almost universally dripping wet and very cold owing to the drastic cuts in coal, gas and electricity. Extremely difficult choices had to be made.

Hudson had a Dutch intelligence officer working for him, who turned out to be most efficient and pleasant. He had been doing his conscription service in the Dutch Navy in Indonesia when the war broke out. On return to Holland, when the country was overrun, he had been snapped up by the Germans. On the march to a labour camp he threw himself into a ditch and escaped. Posing as under-age he was left as a student in a university, while living at home with his mother and sister. After some months he at last managed to get in touch with an underground resistance movement but, much to his chagrin, he was left as a train watcher for months on end. At last he was promoted to an active cell and, sooner than he had anticipated, he was selected by lot to execute a Dutch collaborator, the interpreter to the town's German commandant. The German commandant, accompanied by his interpreter, left his office almost every day at precisely 12.45 p.m. to walk down the street towards the German officers' mess. At the mess entrance the commandant always paused at least momentarily to receive the interpreter's salute and return it. The plan was that at this moment the executioner would swoop by on his bicycle and fire a shot with his revolver. He had been warned by his chief that he must shoot to kill and must on no account wound. He must therefore fire at the victim's head and not at his body. This rule was apparently strictly observed in all 'executions'. It was a nerve-wracking task, but after two dress rehearsals, the plan worked to perfection. The interpreter was killed and the young Dutchman escaped to his house where he found, to his astonishment, that his mother was already a fully paid-up member of the Resistance and had been passing information to the British by radio for months. Eventually the young man escaped to the British lines where he joined the British Army and, after the war, returned to Holland in British uniform as an intelligence officer, and thence to Iserlohn.

One of Hudson's more unpleasant responsibilities lay in the de-Nazification process. He had to deal with appeals from decisions by the officials directly responsible. Every adult German had to complete a long questionnaire on his activities during the entire Hitler regime. Penalties for false answers were very severe indeed. Certain checks were made, but, in addition, the reports of informers were accepted and encouraged and their allegations sifted. Personal vendettas, business advantage and all the lowest and crudest weaknesses of human nature were at some time reflected in these reports. Charges and counter charges overlaid each other, and the only question often seemed to be who was the greater liar? All ex-officers had their accounts frozen. As they were not allowed to employ labour, or to have a bank account, they were reduced to earning their living as manual labourers or in very lowly clerical or other work.

De-Nazification acted as a physical and moral wet blanket which lay heavily on the undernourished, under-housed people in the cold winter of 1946/7. The argument that the Germans deserved all they got, and that they had brought it all on themselves, seemed just futile. If we meant to punish them we should declare our intention and get on with it, but on the contrary our policy was to rehabilitate the German economy in order to enable them to pay for some of the damage they had wrought and to re-establish trade for the benefit of Europe as a whole. Our methods did little to assist this.

Hudson was a personal friend of the Chief British Commissioner in Germany, General Sir Brian Robertson. On one occasion he went to stay with him in Berlin.

The Robertsons were a happy family and an energetic one. Besides riding before breakfast, tours of the town and dinner parties, he allowed me to accompany him to a four-power International Meeting. The four Chiefs sat with their staffs on the four sides of a square table within which sat the stenographers typing the speeches in slow motion, in shorthand, easily keeping up with the speakers. Only the Chiefs spoke and it was Robertson's turn to act as chairman.

The agenda included consideration of the treatment to be accorded to Germans condemned at the Nuremberg trials. There was much argument as to what exactly was meant by 'solitary confinement'. The French understood it to mean that the prisoner should be in a cell by himself, but that he should be allowed to speak to other prisoners during exercise or during other special periods. The Americans and British agreed that life imprisonment in strictly solitary confinement would be inhuman. The Russian was asked his opinion. He stated briefly that his country would have shot the lot if they had had their way; since this had not been done, as they had wished, they could take no further interest in what happened.

The meeting was a cheerful one and at one point the whole room burst into loud and delighted laughter. The question of the censorship of inter-zone mail was being discussed. During the discussion it became obvious to everyone the Frenchman had dozed off. Robertson asked him point blank if he thought postcards should be included in the regulations as drafted for the approval of the meeting.

The Frenchman woke up with a start and blinked.

'Postcards, General,' Robertson said again. 'What about them?'

The General still looked rather dazed and puzzled but he quickly brightened.

'Picture postcards,' he said, 'should not be censored.'

The cheers of approval at first perturbed him but he quickly recovered and joined in.

After a few months, Hudson was promoted to Kreis Group Commander. Then he was offered further promotion but, 'I firmly refused to stay on for the reason that the whole atmosphere was too depressing and I hated living amongst people whom I could not like, for the Germans seemed to me a very unlovable people. Being parted from my wife, too, seemed senseless and unnecessary.' He went out to Germany in November 1946 and returned to England for good in May 1947.

TWELVE

· · · · · · · · · · · · · ·

Retirement

Hudson did not see his final return to England in 1947, aged
55, as a coda of little significance when compared to the very
full and varied experiences he had had thus far. He saw it as a
new beginning. He worked hard in his small wood, he joined
the St John Ambulance Brigade, becoming Devonshire County
Commissioner and eventually Knight of the Order of St John.
He wrote poetry about many aspects of life. The view from the
window of his new house and an elegy for an aunt are among
the poems he wrote at this time.

View from my Window

Can heaven be more beautiful than this broad sweep
Of England's countryside? These hills diaphanous
Whose curtained ridges rise in ordered precedence
In changing light with baffling inexactitude
And as the sinking sun reflected in the clouds
Throws darkening purple shadows, a distant golden
   cornfield claims
My roving eye. A patch of brilliant emerald green
Below succeeds, and in the sky an ever widening gap
Of azure blue is fringed with gold tipped creamy cloud.
The while in peaceful clumps the dark green trees
   are massed and spaced
Within the valley's bowl with perfect artistry.
A farm with gabled roofs half buried in a shroud
   of trees
Proclaims itself by smoke, a column swelling out
To float uncertain in the evening still.

The Happy Passing
(on the death of an aunt)

The aged lady white and frail and worn
Is lying there, the while her life with slow
But certain ebb prolongs its final flow
Towards the unknown sea; and they who mourn
But stand and sadly wait the coming dawn.
'When will her spirit pass with all the love
She showered upon the world from that great trove
Her lion heart,' they ask themselves forlorn.

The whispers low they bend to hear the voice
They love once more, for now the time has come –
The end – then very clear 'Had I the choice
Not otherwise than this would I go home' –
She said – and thus the aged lady died
And thus another spirit death defied.

He kept his sense of humour, laughing until the tears streamed down his face as he told of an instance before the war. When travelling up to Scotland with his family to fish on Loch Maree, they stopped for the night at a small, very Scottish, temperance hotel (there were no motorways in those days). The atmosphere was highly depressing as conversation among the clientele was confined to a few whispered confidences supplemented by disapproving looks in all directions. He couldn't stand it any longer and, thinking his wife Gladys was in the lounge, he opened the door and crawled in on all fours barking like a small dog. 'Woof, woof, woof,' he went and, still on all fours, approached a chair from which appeared a female leg. He slowly sniffed up it to find himself confronted by a totally terrified woman, transfixed by the certainty that she was in the presence of a dangerous lunatic. The situation was not improved by the only words Hudson could think of to say in the circumstances: 'I'm sorry, I thought you were my wife.'

He also described an incident before the war when he and Gladys were leaving Rome by train. Just before the train left, a sizable German lady sat down in the chair opposite them clutching a large paper bag out of which she extracted a magnificent cream bun. As the train began to move, she took a bite out of it but the cream was sour; she grimaced and threw it out of the window to hit the stationmaster, ultra smart in his uniform, marching down the platform, full in the face. It was too late for the train to be stopped and it gathered speed. The German lady was terrified, thinking of the fate which would undoubtedly have been hers in Germany if she had assaulted a uniformed stationmaster. In fact nothing happened, even when the train reached the next station.

Hudson described with sympathy an encounter experience he had had probably many years before with one woman:

Pride

We, my friend and I
Met a harlot in the street
She looked so wan. Her feet
Were sore, she said, from walking
'Why do we stand here talking.
My friend and I
Between us share a cosy flat.'
'And where,' demanded I, 'is that?'
My friend said, drawing me aside,
'Don't be a fool. Have you no pride?'
'None. She is starving.' I replied.

We, my friend and I,
Arranged to go but not to stay
To let them earn their pay.
'We live here happily,' she said,
'My friend has gone to bed,
I'll call her in.'
Then in the passage blistering
Reproof, we heard them whispering.
'Coffee? Beer? There isn't any.'
'Biscuits?' 'Just a few, not many.'
'I haven't got a bloody penny.'

We, my friend and I,
When we later reached the street
Declared we hoped to meet
No more such bitter scorning.
We wouldn't stay 'til morning!
'My friend and I,'
The woman said, 'would rather die
Than take your dirty money. Why
Did you come?' She swore we lied

And when we looked aghast, she cried
'Do you suppose we have no pride?'

And another:

The Girl in Front in a London Street

Why do you hurry so with springy haste
Of youthfulness, and hair that lifts and falls
Shorn of its natural length. So trim a waist
So elegant a back. What is it calls?
Why cheat this summer eve by being so brisk?
Perhaps your lover waits, and you are late
To make your rendezvous. To see your face
I'd have to hurry after you. I'd hate
To spoil your dainty charm so just in case
You're plain, I'll saunter on, and take no risk.

Like many men who have survived the trenches of the First
World War and the constant loss of comrades there, Hudson
was very cautious about making close friends; in fact, he really
did not have any. People liked him; he was the most modest
hero, if that was what he was, but he was not a very social
person. His experiences in the First World War led him to avoid
any very close bond with other human beings, male or female.
There were two exceptions to this. First, of course, his wife
Gladys who was devoted to him and bore all his tribulations
with stoical grace, giving him succour and total support when
it was needed, without in any way being dominated by him.
She, too, was a very powerful character. She was also, perhaps,
a little puritanical at times, due no doubt to her North Country
background. Even so, she was able to see the funny side of
most situations.

In Hudson's later years, when the author was around – and this was not very often – they were 'best friends'. They were able to talk freely about anything, to play golf and tennis together and generally to enjoy each other's company enormously.

Meanwhile, in 1949, Hudson's next trial took place when his house was burnt down and he lost virtually everything in it. He and Gladys were asleep in their bedroom in the middle of the night when they were awoken by a loud crackling noise. They realised to their horror that there was a fire in the library beneath them where Hudson had been smoking a cigarette before going to bed. They escaped with their lives and nothing else except a portrait of their son John.

Probably for the first time in his life Hudson had been suffering from bouts of depression, as there seemed little left for him to do. The burning down of his house and the loss of virtually all his possessions, far from being a debilitating experience was the exact opposite. The challenge of finding a new house, furnishing it and starting again was most timely. He bought a largish manor house and garden in a village and again became a feature of Devonshire life – Deputy Lieutenant of the County, Justice of the Peace and so on.

He was assiduous in his duties as a magistrate and as County Commissioner of the St John's Ambulance Brigade. At heart, though, he remained a rebel, never seeing himself as a member of the establishment. However, he did attend the review by the Queen of holders of the Victoria Cross in Hyde Park on 26 June 1956.

Hudson's wife Gladys was very musical and played the piano with great passion. Hudson loved listening to great music as this poem makes clear.

Wireless. A Winter's Night

I am possessed
With melody
Lulled
And soothed.
Then gripped and smashed
And torn apart with torrent sound.
As suddenly
Dismissed again and carried back to quietude.
Then bursting out
The drums assault
My ears
Merciless.
They rise and fall,
As bric-a-brac on breaking waves
Is toss'd, then drawn
Back to the boiling cauldron of tumultuous seas.

I sit worn out
Limp as a rag
Broken
Exhausted.
The fire burns low.
My thoughts run riot in my head
My body's tense.
Worn out, yet clinging desperately to ecstasy.

He became very interested in chess and produced a number of chess problems of various kinds, some of which were printed in chess magazines. He wrote his 730-page journal. In addition he wrote two radio plays, ten short stories and many reflections on a multitude of secular subjects. He tried unsuccessfully to have the plays produced, but this did not seem to bother him much, as he wrote for himself.

He attended church regularly. The church was attached to the manor house where he lived, but his religion was of the romantic rather than the doctrinaire kind. He distrusted the certainties of some approaches to religion while being deeply affected by the story of the life and death of Jesus Christ.

Good Friday

Gently, Ah gently let them take him down
And gently, gently, lay him on the ground.
He was my son, good Sir, and I alone
Can claim the final right this dreadful mound,
This Golgotha, this place of skulls, has left
To me, a loving mother's right to weep.
I bore him, Sir, and if the scorn of men
Was his the pain is mine. The world may sleep
No less tonight because he died but then
They knew him not as I his mother knew.
His death has proved to me his perfect love,
His life will ever be unending pride
To me. Would I had seen the Holy Dove
Descend in that last hour, then had I cried,
The moment that he passed, my last farewell.
Leave me one hour to pray by him this night,
Still they can bury him before the day
The sun shall never more give him the sight
He loved, the rising sun. He used to say

'Behold the lilies of the field. Are one
Of you arrayed as one of these?' How good
He was I know, even the thief had guessed,
For in his dying pains he understood.
Yet, knowing not, grant me this last request,
Good Sir, you see he was my son.

When the author departed as a soldier for Malaya in 1951, out of the blue arrived the following remarkable poem from my father:

For My Son

God-speed my son, I would not hold you back
Had I the power, and yet I grieve that you should go.
God-speed across the world. You nothing lack
If thoughts of mine can give the fiery sunset's glow,
The dawn, the midday heat, the evening star,
The gifts of love and strength I would were ever thine.
God-speed in all your enterprise afar.
I do not seek to counsel you, no words of mine
Can help to keep you on a chosen way.
The pattern of a life alone can teach
To other men what they should do or say
Or guard against or spur themselves to reach.
Take then from mine the best my pattern gives
And for the rest I trust you'll give me tolerance
Perhaps a smile.
That other one who lives
Again in you, her pattern too affords a chance
To pick upon. No better wish have I
Than that you seek to take from her her pattern's best.
These gifts we cannot alter nor deny,
Our threads are woven and our patterns made, no quest

Can change them now. For you your life's design
Can still be spun as you would later have it be.
Watch well the golden thread and mark the line
It takes. Preserve it in your inner sanctuary.
That thread of faith must in your pattern lie
Buried at times by thoughtless word or selfish deed
But ever there and you until you die
Can save or tarnish it as you may will. God-speed.

He died in April 1959 while on holiday in the Scilly Islands. He was 66 years and 11 months old.

How, then, does one sum up the life of Charles Hudson?

His military career had two totally opposite aspects: his fighting ability and his eventual failure on the Army ladder of promotion. There can be no doubt about ability to fight, his courage and his leadership qualities in war. As far as his promotion was concerned, his early advancement over the heads of almost all his contemporaries and many of his seniors was justified both in France in the First World War and in Belgium and France in the Second World War. On the other hand, he was sacked as a divisional commander, never regained his rank of major-general in spite of a number of near misses. He finished his Army career in 1946 as a brigadier – the rank he had held in 1938. He did not, or would not, conform to what was expected of him in the higher ranks of the Army. He was a rebel in almost every sense of that rather ambiguous word. He seemed to enjoy disagreeing with established opinions, but was not very adept either at choosing the moment to speak out or at expressing himself in the company of his superiors.

Throughout his life, he searched for beauty. His early attachment to Walt Whitman was unusual for a young man of his background. He found beauty in the poems he read and in those he wrote for himself, which he never tried to have published. He kept his reflections to himself. He did not care much about what other people thought of him. Despite his achievements, he was very modest and able to find solace in humour and his loving wife who, to a great degree, shared his outlook on life.

Where did all these characteristics come from? His was a conventional background – no hint of rebellion there. One of the great mysteries of the twentieth century was how and why so many young Britons were prepared to die in the trenches in spite of the obvious fact that many of their sacrifices were in vain. There will never be a definitive answer: history is eternally mysterious. How can anyone put themselves in the place of someone else now, let alone decades or centuries past?

Hudson loved his country, as did millions of Britons, and this was part of his and of many others' motivation. Duty and Honour, those slightly dated concepts, were instilled in him as indeed they were in virtually all his contemporaries of the officer class by the public school system. These convictions played a part in his motivation, as did the almost school-boyish enthusiasm for crawling about no man's land in the First World War. But as far as he was concerned there was more to it than that.

Hudson was born with an innate self-confidence. As a young boy he rode up to the poachers on his father's estate and demanded what they were doing, to his own immediate discomfiture.

It was his ghastly experiences at his preparatory school, however, which undoubtedly played a major part in his character. He had lost all self-esteem, but managed to regain it at his public school, Sherborne. Having been through that experience once, he was not going to repeat it, even in wartime. As far as his poetry is concerned, the schoolmaster Trevor Dennis opened his eyes to a fascinating world, with all its mystery and beauty.

On leaving school Hudson was not going to be beholden to anyone, let alone his brother, so off he went to Ceylon in spite of great doubts about the philistine situation he expected to encounter, and indeed did.

The rest of Charles Hudson's life falls into a pattern which he had established in early youth: a refusal to be bound by convention, as a result of his early experiences which had taught him to ignore and indeed to distrust it. His leadership qualities: his sublime courage, his refusal to obey what he conceived to be stupid orders and his bloody-minded behaviour to his superiors on many occasions. One example of this stubborness was when as divisional commander he insisted on court-martialling a battalion commanding officer under his command for what turned out to be a perfectly understandable action.

As for the meaning of the word courage, in Charles Hudson's case it amounted to the possession of considerable will power to overcome the fear which deeply affected him, like virtually everybody else, in both world wars. Lord Moran in his book *Anatomy of Courage* describes how, as a doctor in the trenches in the First World War, he observed that this attribute of will power in overcoming fear is gradually eroded as it is used. This did not seem to be the case with Hudson, whose store of courage appeared to be unaffected despite constant use.

Probably the most striking example of his courage, not physical but moral, came when he was asked to give evidence against the corps commander who had sacked him, but refused to do so in spite of hints that if he did so he would regain command of his division. He had given his word not to re-open the matter and that was that. He had the courage to resist the obvious temptation of, as he saw it, dishonest behaviour.

Hudson's great virtue was a determination to take positive action whatever the circumstances in war or peace. His vice was an attraction to confrontation with established convention. The poetic side of his character gave him a sense of perception which enabled him to rise above mundane worries, to keep his all-pervading sense of humour and remain unembittered by apparent failure.

All these attributes – courage, poetic insight, rebelliousness – were combined in his character. Not one of them could have existed without the other two.

He met with Triumph and Disaster and cheated those two imposters just the same.

APPENDIX A

● ●

Citations, Awards and Appointments

CHARLES EDWARD HUDSON, VICTORIA CROSS
Asiago Plateau, Italy, 15 June 1918

CITATION

For most conspicuous bravery and devotion to duty when his battalion was holding the right front sector during an attack on the British Front.

The shelling had been very heavy on the right, the trench destroyed, and considerable casualties had occurred, and all the officers on the spot were killed or wounded. This enabled the enemy to penetrate our front line.

The enemy pushed their advance as far as the support line which was the key to our flank. The situation commanded immediate action. Lieutenant-Colonel Hudson, recognising its gravity, at once collected various headquarter details, such as orderlies, servants, runners etc. and, together with some Allies, personally led them up the hill.

Driving the enemy down hill, towards our front line, he again led a party of about five up the trench, where there were about 200 enemy, in order to attack them from one flank. He then with two men got out of the trench and rushed the position, shouting to the enemy to surrender, some of whom did. He was then severely wounded by a bomb which exploded on his foot. Although in great pain, he gave directions for the counter-attack to be continued, and this was done successfully, about 100 prisoners and six machine-guns being taken.

Without doubt the high courage and determination displayed by Lieutenant-Colonel Hudson saved a serious situation, and had it not been for his quick determination in organising the counter-attack a large number of the enemy would have dribbled through, and counter-attack on a larger scale would have been necessary to restore the situation.

COMPANION OF THE ORDER OF THE BATH 1940
DISTINGUISHED SERVICE ORDER
London Gazette, 16 August 1917

CITATION

For conspicuous gallantry and devotion to duty. During an attack and before the objective was gained, he showed great promptitude and disregard for his own safety in reorganising his battalion and leading it forward to the objective which was secured and consolidated through his successful efforts. He has on many occasions showed capacity of the highest military value, notably in repulsing hostile counter-attacks upon his battalion at a critical moment.

BAR TO DISTINGUISHED SERVICE ORDER
London Gazette, 26 November 1917

CITATION

For conspicuous gallantry and devotion to duty. He was in command of a sector of the front line for several days during an action, and organised and carried out the defence of the position under continuous and violent enemy shelling. It was entirely due to his organisation and personal supervision of the work that the line was able to resist heavy enemy counter-attacks. He showed splendid leadership and great energy and courage.

MILITARY CROSS
London Gazette, 25 November 1916

CITATION

For conspicuous gallantry in action. He led his company with great courage and initiative, capturing two enemy bombing posts. He has on many previous occasions done very fine work.

FRENCH CROIX DE GUERRE AVEC PALME
1916

ITALIAN SILVER MEDAL FOR MILITARY VALOUR
1918

MENTIONED IN DESPATCHES

15 June 1916, 30 May 1916, 21 December 1917, 6 January 1919, 9 July 1919, 3 February 1920

APPOINTMENTS

ADC to King George VI, 1944–6
Justice of the Peace
Knight of Saint John of Jerusalem

APPENDIX B

● ●

Perfect Lines

Charm'd magic casements, opening on the foam
Of perilous seas, in faery lands forlorn.

Keats, 'Ode to a Nightingale'

A savage place! As holy and enchanted
As E'er beneath a waning moon was haunted
By woman wailing for her demon-lover!

Coleridge, 'Kubla Khan'

Or hear old Triton blow his wreathèd horn.

Wordsworth, 'The World'

Whose dwelling is the light of setting suns.

Wordsworth, 'Tintern Abbey'

The moan of doves in immemorial elms
And murmuring of innumerable bees.

Tennyson, 'Come Down, O Maid'

After life's fitful fever he sleeps well.

Shakespeare, Macbeth

The singing masons building roofs of gold.

Shakespeare, Henry V

Pavilioned in splendour and girded with praise.

Sir Robert Grant, Hymn, 'O Worship the King'

Tranquil you lie, your knightly virtue proved.

J.S. Arkright, Hymn, 'O Valiant Hearts'

The uncertain glory of an April day.

Shakespeare, Two Gentlemen of Verona

Life, like a dome of many-coloured glass
Stains the white radiance of Eternity.

Shelley, 'Adonais'

A springful of larks in a rolling cloud.

Dylan Thomas, 'Poem in October'

The holy time is quiet as a nun,
Breathless with adoration.

Wordsworth, Sonnet, 'It is a Beauteous Evening'

The sedge is withered from the lake
And no birds sing.

Keats, 'La Belle Dame sans Merci'

The dragon green, the luminous, the dark,
the serpent haunted sea.

James Elroy Flecker, 'The Gates of Damascus'

Dawn skims the sea with flying feet of gold.

Swinburne

In that dim world between the tides of sleep.

Anon

A rose-red city half as old as time.

Dean Burgeon, 'Petra', Newdigate,
Prize Poem, 1845

By many a temple, half as old as time.

Samuel Rogers, Italy, A Farewell, 1839

APPENDIX C

• • • • • • • • • • • • • • • • • • • •

Newspaper Extracts

EXTRACT FROM *STAR*, LONDON, 31 JANUARY 1938

Major Hudson's Promotion

Another VC, Major C.E. Hudson, has jumped over all the full colonels in the Army List – a feat almost unprecedented in peace time.

Hudson joined the Army as a temporary officer when the war started and had no notion of making it his career until he discovered himself to be a 'born soldier'. He won the VC on the Asiago Plateau in Italy in 1918, by saving a dangerous situation, and now, at the age of 46, he is to commmand the 2nd Infantry Brigade.

This is the Brigade that was rushed off to Palestine in September, 1936, but the various units are now trickling back to Aldershot.

EXTRACT FROM *NATAL MERCURY*, 2 JUNE 1938

Promotion For VCs

Britain's energetic Secretary for War, Mr Leslie Hore-Belisha, seems to have a predilection for men who wear the Victoria Cross. Following his choice of Viscount Gort, VC, as Army Chief, he has singled out other VCs.

A recent promotion is that of Colonel C.E. Hudson, VC, DSO, who was a Ceylon rubber planter before the War.

Mr Hore-Belisha has a real bent for giving a popular flourish to his work. The policy of choosing leaders from among those who have distinguished themselves at war should appeal to the rank and file.

EXTRACT FROM *THE TIMES*, LONDON, 1 FEBRUARY 1938

Major to Brigadier

Major and Brevet Lieutenant-Colonel C.E. Hudson, VC, DSO, MC, who is to command the 2nd Infantry Brigade, does not pass from major to brigadier without having commanded a battalion, for he was commanding the 11th Sherwood Foresters in Italy when he won the V.C. and its Italian equivalent. He joined the Army in 1914 as a temporary second lieutenant and had eight decorations when the War ended.

EXTRACT FROM *MALAY MAIL*, KUALA LUMPUR, 3 JUNE 1938

Colonel Hudson

Colonel C.E. Hudson, who has been hailed as one of Mr Hore-Belisha's best 'discoveries,' must be well-remembered by many in Malaya. This quiet, pleasant little man, who has been honoured with the VC and the DSO was before the War a rubber planter in Ceylon.

Afterwards, from 1929 to 1932, he was in command of the local volunteer forces in Malaya, and was regarded as one of the most brilliant tacticians ever sent out.

On returning home he took up a staff appointment at Sandhurst as a second in command. He is as popular here as he was in the East, which is saying a good deal, and his numerous friends will be pleased at his recognition.

EXTRACT FROM *THE TIMES*, LONDON,

16 NOVEMBER 1938

Tank Divisions

In the November number of the Journal of the Royal United Service Institution appears an article on 'The Tasks of the Army,' by Brevet Lieutenant-Colonel C.E. Hudson, VC, DSO, The King's Own Scottish Borderers.

'Few students of Army organization,' he writes, 'can have failed to read the three articles that recently appeared in *The Times* under the title of "The Tasks of the Army," the manifest end and object of which was to suggest to the public a practical means by which our peace-time Army might be reorganized to meet the conditions, and they could hardly have been more clearly and concisely put. But the suggested measures to attain the desired end seem woefully inadequate.'

While agreeing that an infantry battalion commander is at present overburdened by the number of subordinates whom he must directly command and the complexity of the weapons which he must attempt to control, Colonel Hudson suggests that more fundamental reorganization than the formation of a support battalion in each brigade may be necessary. He points out that modern conditions in civilized warfare have forced upon us a new close combat attack unit, a tank battalion, and he discusses a reorganization, including a new formation, the tank division.

Index